MANDRYKA

MANDRYKA

When First We Met, He Called Me Mandryka

Sebastian Bartók

authorHOUSE®

AuthorHouse™ UK
1663 Liberty Drive
Bloomington, IN 47403 USA
www.authorhouse.co.uk
Phone: 0800.197.4150

Published by AuthorHouse   03/04/2015

ISBN: 978-1-4969-9905-4 (sc)
ISBN: 978-1-4969-9904-7 (hc)
ISBN: 978-1-4969-9906-1 (e)

For Frederic

PROLOGUE

When I was a small-town boy from Austria, I ventured into the next larger town, Munich, across the border in Bavaria, whenever I wanted to enjoy life, since Innsbruck and Salzburg were just as boring as my small town of Kufstein. This became possible for the first time in 1956, after the last Allied French troops left for good in the autumn of 1955.

At home the only entertainment seemed to be the cinema. Unless you were sporty (which I was not) and played football with the other guys, there was nothing else to do. If you were lucky, there was a tête-à-tête in the darkening corners, during the fading light of the day. There were dancing lessons, often with girlfriends, or the spotty, acne marked boys with wallflowers. It was just show, to conform to the restrictive society. These places not only smelled of boredom, but they were an utterly banal collection of motley individuals who watched their neighbours from behind net curtains.

I had to live with a stepfather who played the despot of an impoverished family. I found great solace in reading and buried my head in books, which came mainly from the town's library or from friends. If it hadn't been for that, I would have died of boredom and despair.

I had a number of pen pals who, like me, lived under one or another of the Occupation forces, which happened to be the French in the Austrian Tyrol. The British, French, American, and Russian forces were the occupiers of Austria and Germany, where the Occupation was more restrictive than ours. A few pen pals living in the West I was able to correspond with, but most of those letters were strictly censored. These pen pals kept me busy writing letters, often until midnight.

This was how I happened to get to know Maja, from Finland, and to make my subsequent, innocent approach to the world. Having kept in touch for well over three years and exchanged mountains of pictures, we hatched a plot. Following my bank apprenticeship, we would spend a gap year together. I allowed myself this excursion because I had excellent grades; there would be no shortage of job opportunities for me thereafter. Why should we not enjoy ourselves in the meantime?

Various moonlighting jobs had allowed me to save some money. This would be the longest trip I had ever made on my own. I was quite excited and wondered what her family might say, as well as what my visit had in store for me. When I boarded the train, I was a little more than 17 years old.

Backpackers in Europe were few and far between in those days, and I felt very adventurous. The train from Kufstein on the Austro-German border took me to Munich, then across the length of Germany to Hamburg and on to Copenhagen. I planned all this without any help. I loved the journey, even when the land went flat and dirty with the smoke of the factory chimneys right through the heartland of German industry. Just to be on the train gave me a real sense of freedom.

Keep in mind that up-to-date travel guides were not as readily available in the 1950s as they are today. Nor did we have the Internet. A lot of research had to be done beforehand, most information published before World War II had become unreliable and haphazard. Letters had to be written and routes had to be changed. A lot of planning went into my preparation for the trip.

Changing trains quite often, large sections of the railway had been almost destroyed during the war and detours still had to be made. There was no bridge and tunnel over the Öresund in those days. You had to board a ferry which took you over to Malmö and on to Stockholm by train. The Scandinavian train was far more comfortable than our clapped-out trains in Austria and Germany, which were pieced together from old bits of pre-war stock.

In Stockholm I was a little lost, but eventually found a boarding house where I could spend the night. The next day's ferry took me to Turku, or Åbo as it was called in Swedish, which was widely spoken on the west coast of Finland.

Little did I know that, above and beyond their function of making the crossing from Sweden to Finland, these ferries were nicknamed "sailing brothels" among those in the know. In the 1950s, the adult male population in Scandinavia was outnumbered by its female counterpart by a ratio of almost three to one due to the casualties incurred during World War II. This ferry was a haven for men. You could have almost any girl you wanted, so long as she was alone. Many used this ferry to have a sexual encounter and get properly sloshed. I found myself in a cabin with an attractive young Swedish girl. I have no idea how I got there ... and no further description is necessary, other than it turned out to be very pleasant.

At the time, alcohol in Sweden and Finland was very expensive. Prices were so high that ordinary people could only afford it now and then, both countries had also a high per capita number of asylums – but no one likes to talk about those. Illegal breweries flourished, but if you got caught, the fines were more than stiff. Apart from that, the Finns were about the most hospitable nation you could meet.

On one occasion I did not arrive in Kuopio in the lake district, which was my intended destination, but in Tampere on the western side of Finland. "Well," I said to myself, "Sebastian, you will just have to rough it and hope that the waiting room will stay open until the first train in the morning."

No sooner had I installed myself on a bench, arranging my rucksack as a headrest and spreading some of my clothes to cover the rest of my body, than the stationmaster appeared with a bunch of keys and indicated I had to leave, since he had to lock up. Now what? Given my non-existent Finnish, I simply showed him my ticket. He understood that I had taken the wrong direction at the last junction.

He also understood that I was stuck. He took me back to his house, where his wife rustled up an extra portion of dinner and let me use their telephone to tell my friends that I had taken the wrong train and would not arrive until the following afternoon. They showed me their guest room and the bathroom. The following morning after showering and a hearty cooked breakfast the stationmaster brought back a friend or neighbour who spoke English. "Thank God", I learned where to change to arrive safely at the station where my friends were waiting for me. Then we all shook hands and said goodbye.

Let us return to the story of my youthful journey and first steps on Finnish soil. Coming off the ferry, I found a boulder where I could sit down and peruse the map of Turku which I had bought on the ship. The strong smell of the pine forest at the entrance to the town was overwhelming. When the sun came out to dry the night's dew on the branches, it gave them an even more potent smell. I felt extremely comfortable and at home with the well-known scent of the trees. I was happy with my progress so far, but was still trying to find out where I was in relation to the town.

A young lady on a bike stopped and asked if she could be of any help. She was studying at the university and offered to take me to their day centre, where I met a lot of students who were studying English and German. Some of the students found German particularly difficult and made me do a mock A-level exercise, which turned out not to be as bad as expected. Suddenly the day had vanished, and it was time to go to the railway station, to say *goodbye* to the young people, all of whom came along to wish me luck in my endeavours.

Finally I arrived in Rovaniemi, where Maja and her family lived. Her two brothers came with her to the station to welcome me. She was just the kind of girl I could fall in love with. She was even better looking than I expected judging by the pictures she had sent to me over the last few years.

The family lived in a white clapboard house on the periphery of old Rovaniemi, which was similar to many of the houses in the area. You had to remember its exact location or you might be in for an uncomfortable surprise. After a few days I felt it would be appropriate to have a stroll through the neighbourhood and get acquainted with the old town, only to get hopelessly lost. No matter what I did, I always came back to the wrong house. I seemed to be in trouble, since none of the people I encountered spoke either English or German. Warily I approached an elderly lady, who I thought should know the area, but to no avail. She also did not speak any foreign language. She gestured she was going to take me to another house. She kept apologizing for not being able to help – at least, that was what I understood.

But there was something strange about her Finnish. Here and there, Hungarian words were interwoven. I took my courage into both hands and asked if she by any chance spoke Hungarian. The Finnish and the Hungarian languages are grammatically similar, but the spoken words are quite different. Linguists consider the Finno-Ugric languages as originating in Mongolian tribal languages; one tribe settled in Finland and another in Hungary.

Her face lit up and she answered in perfect Hungarian. When she was a young girl, her parents had sent her to the Liszt Conservatoire in Budapest to study the piano. Hungarian was the only foreign language she spoke very well. After ending her studies, she remained in Budapest, partly because she was unable to go home during the war and the ensuing occupation, and partly because she enjoyed teaching young and gifted students until her retirement. Somewhere there was also a man involved, either a sweetheart or a husband.

But what a chance! Here we were in the middle of winter, in mountains of snow, and I had found somebody who could speak Hungarian. I was still quite fluent, since my Hungarian mother stubbornly refused to speak or write to me in German. As long as she lived, the situation did not change.

That incident happened many months before an unforgettable midsummer's night. A platform of timber was erected in the fields, kitted out with harvest bales of wheat, and vegetables neatly arranged in baskets. The Finnish flag was flying over the canopy. There were benches for the participants to sit on, and the old folks had tables and chairs right behind. They would not stay very long.

The musicians warmed up and started playing. Sibelius might have had something to say about beginning the evening with his "Finlandia"; maybe he even participated in such events when he was young. The food offered was smorgasbord sandwiches of a substantial kind, and for a while everybody tucked in. All the young people were waiting for the old folks to leave, so they could let their hair down without parental control.

It was true, legal alcohol was very expensive in Finland. There was a lot of homemade vodka, to which I attributed the heightened atmosphere. Everybody was drinking – not just soft drinks, but something else as well, which the barmaids kept pouring out of unlabelled bottles. These unfortunate girls got their jobs on the sidelines because they looked like the Rhine Maidens in *Das Rheingold* and were extremely ugly.

During the first round of drinks, it seemed no one dared to make a start. The band did their best with familiar songs of the fifties and some American folk tunes. Finally the dancing started. It was announced that the ladies would make their choices of partners first, since there were far more of them than men or boys in their late teens. Soon scuffles broke out among the female sorority, each trying to nick the other's beau. You could feel the tension in the air; it reminded me of animals during the mating season. The sun was still shining near to midnight. Tempers frayed, and I was quite amused by the whole spectacle. Maja had had enough when quite a few of the young flaxen-haired beauties made a beeline for me and tried to drag me away. She feigned a headache, which I thought was just embarrassment. The scene was reminiscent of Tennessee Williams' *Cat on a Hot Tin Roof.*

As the weeks progressed, Maja and I got even closer, and I thought for a while we would make a life together. Innocent youth! Maja became pregnant. When it could no longer be concealed, she had to confess to her parents. They were not enchanted – they were simply livid, which is putting it politely. The whole family was brought together round the fireplace in the middle of the living room, where we sat most evenings in our rocking chairs, saying very little. But this evening the atmosphere had changed. It was hostile. I did not relish all the shouting. It was fuelled by anger, and I could not follow exactly what was going on. But the body language and the increasing noise were very unpleasant to witness.

When we were alone later on, Maja explained to me that we would have to pack that night. One of her brothers drove us to the station the following morning with the whole family's blessings, never to return. They gave us some money to see us through the next few months, and thereafter we were to fend for ourselves.

By that time of year, it was dark for almost twenty-four hours a day. We found ourselves on the train and then the ferry to Stockholm. I thought I would have some explaining to do to my parents. To give us some time, Maja and I returned to the Stockholm boarding house where I had stayed just over a year before, at the beginning of my visit. Then I had everything going for me, and now I was becoming a father at the tender age of 18.

I do not know how to describe our agony and fear of what might happen to us. I thought of Thomas Hardy's novel *Far from the Madding Crowd*, in which Fanny the servant girl was made pregnant by the ruthless husband of Bathsheba, and the girl and baby died in the workhouse. Thank God we did not live in the times of a hundred years ago. Was it fate that I read the novel again? This time in English and not in a German translation. But how could I know what was going to happen to us in a short while? God has strange ways of directing our lives. My maternal grandmother, who was deeply religious, maintained that if God closed a door, he would open a window elsewhere.

Maja became very ill and had to be taken to hospital. After a full investigation, the surgeon told me that the baby was in the wrong position and there would have to be a caesarean birth, to save hopefully both or at least one of them. What a misfortune. We were hardly out of our own infancy, and now we were to have a baby born in a foreign land. Where to go from here?

I rang my mother. She told me that she had had words with my stepfather, who was far more concerned about me repaying the money I owed him for my schooling and the bank apprenticeship. Then, and only then, we might stay with them for a while until I was able to provide for my own family.

Mother also told me that, whatever happened, she knew a way out as far as the money was concerned. But since it was an affair, she would not like my stepfather to know, she would tell me as soon as we saw each other again. No more was said but I knew I could rely on her. The second advice was, to stay away from my stepfather and live in another town until everything was sorted out.

I thought, "Well, Sebastian, you have made a proper mess of your life. When most people are just starting out, you will have to care for a young family." Payback time and pain had started rather early. But as I said, destiny often goes different ways.

Maja never recovered from the complicated birth of our son and died a few weeks later. The efficiency of the Swedish social services made things easier. Although the Swedish parliament had reduced the age of majority from 21 to 18, I feared I could have been prosecuted in Finland if Maja's parents had started an action against me, and I could have had a one or two year prison sentence. However, our son was taken away from me as soon as Maja had gone. He was given up for adoption with the proviso that I never try to find him.

A few years went by. Only Mum knew where I was, and she kept it to herself. Just as later on she would not let on that we were going on an epic journey. Eventually I decided to work for a bank in Freiburg, in the Black Forest, which I hated from the beginning.

Yes, there were other girls in my life. But I only recall a few; the rest vanished as if they had never happened. There was one girl, Renie from Hamburg, who touched me a little closer. But I would not easily get over Maja's death and the loss of our baby boy, given up for adoption and never seen again.

CHAPTER 1

Újvidék

Újvidék was the capital of the autonomous state Vojvodina, as well as my place of birth, in the federation of Yugoslavia, staunchly Hungarian and left pretty much as it had been for hundreds of years, until Tito died and the Serbs started taking over.

When I returned from Stockholm, and had settled in Freiburg in the Black Forest my mother came to see me. Finally she told me some of the story about herself and my real father. The year I was born was 1942, on a cold January day. My mother had rekindled an affair with her childhood sweetheart upon his return to Újvidék in the spring 1941. He did not want to stay in Budapest and get involved in yet more shooting and killing. He was also on a spying mission, since he spoke all three languages common of the Vojvodina. The Ustacha of Croatia and the Partisans of Serbia were on his trail, and where better to go into hiding than in your own backyard?

One night, shots rang out in front of our house. Mother's lover had been assassinated. There was a lot of speculation, but no one knew for certain the truth about who shot him. When I was born, he had already been dead for six months. Some sniper shot him in the dark, and even Mother could not find out what had happened that night.

Friends told me much later that Mother had started ailing mentally from that time, and never got over his death. Maybe that tells you a little about her and her personality, why she kept everybody at arm's length and became like an icon with the face of an angel, unable to show joy or pain.

1

I would have liked to have loved her, but she could never show any love to her children either. She remained remote, distant, with her pretty, dark, Mongolian eyes.

Now, in Freiburg, she indicated why she wanted to see me, and that we were going on an epic journey. She wanted me to accompany her.

"Where to?"

"Újvidék."

"What did you say, you said we are going to Újvidék? I doubt we can get a visa."

"Nonsense," she said. "Just leave that part to me. Pack now, there's a good boy. We will take the first train from Freiburg and head towards Munich early tomorrow morning."

"And then?"

"We stay the night in Munich and make our way to the consulate in the morning. I will deal with the application myself. I promise you, you will be on the night train with me to Belgrade and further on to Újvidék."

I knew better than to disagree with her when she was in a mood like that. Arriving at the consulate, there was the usual security guard yawning and dead bored. He told us that no visas would be issued on that day, and we ought to go home and come back tomorrow.

Well, you should have seen Mum. She would not have it. She went through the security door and on to the consul's office in his private quarters. I had not known until then that her Serbo-Croat was so good that she could pick a fight with the consul. We were out, with visas, by lunchtime. On the train later, I could not believe that this was my serene mother, the iconic Madonna, opposite me.

In the meantime, I rang Maria from Oberaudorf, a friend of mine who had been born on the Austro-German border (in the same place where Wernher von Braun was born). I had made a few bicycle tours round Lake

Constance with her. She lived in Munich now and had time to have early supper with us.

Not many passengers joined us in Munich for the long journey. Up and down the train wound through the mountains to the spa town of Bad Gastein. At some point the heating cut out. If Mother had not taken her big, warm fur coat, it would have been much worse, because we were held up for hours on the border with Yugoslavia. Finally they found an engine that could take us to Jesenice, and we started to move through the mountains of Slovenia to the next stop, Ljubljana. From there on, it was on its way to Zagreb, called Agram when it was part of the Habsburg Empire, and on to the Yugoslav plains.

Since Grandpa and Grandma were still alive, of course Mother wanted to see them very much and catch up on the years they had lost. But the visit had another purpose as well, which benefited not only mother but also my grandparents and myself. When things got nasty during the war, she had some valuable jewellery and she bought more – gold and gems and pearls. Before she left town in 1944, she went out to the family farm, telling no one, not even her parents, and buried the loot in the former flower and vegetable garden. She had measured the spot without leaving any signs. Only she knew the location, about two feet down. And there they were!

While Mother was having a heart to heart with her mother, Grandpa took me to visit all the near and distant relatives in the village. We drank a lot of *palinka* (clear schnapps) made from cherries. We got home plastered, and I thought the two women were going to commit a double homicide.

During the week we were there, both ladies were busy giving the jewellery a new home in Mother's fur coat's lining. We had only been given a two-week visa, and we were shadowed by the Yugoslav secret service wherever we went.

This was the only time I saw Mother nostalgic. When we arrived in Újvidék, there were still fiacres – horse-drawn carriages – waiting for the trains, which never arrived, bar the daily shuttle from Belgrade. We took a fiacre and went past my birthplace, an art deco building with a clothes shop on the ground floor and living quarters on the first and second floors. It also had a roof garden. It stood almost next to the post office, which still bore in gold letters the sign "Magyar Király Posta", as well as the station, which was still called "Újvidék Vasútállomás".

Before we continued to the village where Mother's parents lived, still in the old farmhouse, we stopped at the Catholic cathedral, where we both lit a candle for my dead father. I saw a few tears rolling down Mother's cheeks, but she quickly regained her composure and we continued our journey.

Our family home had been built during the belle époque and was designed by a very prominent Serb architect, whose daughter was an English teacher in Újvidék. She used to spend some of the winter at the Winter Palace in Luxor, where we met years later. When we saw each other again, she brought a book along with her. In it were all the prominent buildings her father had designed, including our art nouveau home, pictured and discussed in detail. And as I had promised her, I brought quite a collection of photographs from my first visit. We used to meet in Luxor every year, but this tradition ended suddenly when a group of Swiss tourists was murdered on the steps of the temple dedicated to Hatshepsut, the most successful female pharaoh ever to rule Egypt.

My visit with Mother went only too quickly. We had to say goodbye to my grandparents and relatives, board the train, and be on our way back to Austria. As we packed, my mother stuffed cigarettes and booze in the corners of our suitcases. This puzzled me until we arrived in Jesenice, the border town of Yugoslavia. Then it dawned on me that there was a good reason for her strange behaviour. The border control officers were so busy digging for the cigarettes and the alcohol that they did not bother to search us and see if we carried anything in the lining of our clothes or pockets. The whistle went again, and soon we were on our way to Villach, the Austrian side of the border with the jewellery intact.

Mother was very generous to me. No one knew what was going on. The old man was taking the waters in a spa town. My older half-brother had gone off on a bike tour with some of his mates, and my half-sister was travelling with a school friend and parents in the Provence. Since we were never a close family, telephoning was rarely on the agenda.

Returning to Freiburg in the Black Forest, I met Renie from Hamburg again. She was holidaying with her mother nearby, as she did once or twice a year. It was a bit of a *liebelei* (dalliance), but we both knew it would not last.

Renie was the secretary of an important man in the music business. She invited me to come to Hamburg in the late summer of 1960, where the Beatles gave their legendary concert on 17 August at the Indra Club on the Grosse Freiheit Strasse. They played and sang to very great acclaim. I managed to travel to Hamburg and see them, courtesy of Renie's boss. The two months they played there were a sell-out and did not disappoint anyone who was a fan of early rock. For the first time in my life, I saw teenyboppers, many past their sell-by dates, screaming their hearts out. You could call it mass hysteria, often put on just so that they could boast to their friends that they were there.

CHAPTER 2

Mandryka

Aber der Richtige wenns einen gibt für mich auf dieser Welt, der wird auf einmal dastehen, da vor mir und wird mich anschaun und ich ihn, und keine Zweifel werden sein und keine Fragen.

The one who's right for me, if there is one for me in all this world, will stand before me. There he will be, his eyes upon me, mine on him, and no more doubting will remain and no more asking.

—Arabella, from the opera by Richard Strauss,
Libretto by Hugo von Hofmannsthal

It was a beautiful summer's day when I came back to Munich in 1963, enrolling for two terms at the college for hotel management in Tegernsee, Bavaria. I financed my studies with whatever work I could find in the hotel where I was going to complete my practicum. In the little spare time I had, I also embarked on the study of advanced English. English language skills would enable me, when the time came, to look for a post anywhere in the world.

But first I had to relax and shake off my life in Freiburg. None of my half siblings had any leanings toward the fine arts or classical music. There was so much going on in Munich: the opera, classical concerts, and many galleries to visit. But time was running out and soon I had to start my second apprenticeship. Yet I had decided well; the hotel was a very friendly family business, with a lot of pleasant regulars, mostly from upper Italy, the region around Milan.

One evening I was sitting on a bar stool in a new Schwabing disco, surveying the lively scene around me. The young people were enjoying themselves to the tunes of rock music on the dance floor, and the flirting that could be felt all around electrified the atmosphere. Among the guests were a few well-known stars and starlets. It was not surprising there were good-looking people having a great time. If I had been sensible, I would have gone to the hotel and straight to bed, since it was one o'clock in the morning and I had a very early start.

Suddenly the door of the bar swung open. In swept a young blond man with an entourage of about ten people. Everybody turned round, and the girl next to me raved about his good looks. He was attired in a herringbone jacket, an Oxford blue button-down shirt, a university tie, flannel trousers, and desert boots. A short time later, I learned that this was the very English way of dressing smart yet casual when going out to a bar crawl or an informal dinner. (I, being fond of clothes, later copied the style, adding a blazer and a clan check jacket.)

The group consisted of youthful members of both sexes. There was only one older man with them, sporting dyed-black hair. He did not seem to belong, yet he kept the motley group in check and reminded me very much of the character Gustav von Aschenbach in Thomas Mann's novel *Death in Venice*. They were obviously out for a night of fun.

After a while, they swept out of the disco just the way they had made their entrance. By chance I overheard where they were going next. I decided to follow. Never mind the early start in the morning. I often got to work after having barely enough time for a shower, a change into my uniform, and a cup of strong coffee.

Keeping at a distance, I shadowed the group from bar to bar. Goodness knows how many there were in Munich in those days. Eventually I managed to manoeuvre a near bump into the blond boy. Looking at me, he remarked tartly that he had noticed me following the party. I must have turned crimson and uncomfortable. All I could do was ask him, as casually as possible, whether he would like a drink.

It was just like two sparks fused. With too much ado, he quite nonchalantly replied, "If you must," just as Sebastian Flyte might have done, outrageously, in *Brideshead Revisited*.

My mind was in turmoil. Had I fallen in love with another young man? Was this what I was looking for? It seemed to be a fatal attraction.

The encounter was rather stiff, formal, and inquisitive. Our lives seemed to have had a very similar pattern which started for both of us in distant lands, not far removed from each other and both previously part of the Austro-Hungarian Empire. This would have never been the case if Frederic and his family, part of the German-speaking minority, had not been shown the door by the Czechs – virtually kicked out of Bohemia. As for me and Mother and the rest of the family, we had been forced to flee the Hungarian province of Vojvodina because Mother was married to a man of Austro-German origin. Frederic and his family managed to go farther west, but my family had stayed in occupied Austria.

Leave it to fate or destiny; Frederic and I had managed to have this meeting in the aftermath of insufferable pain and sorrow. Now we were looking forward to a future we had never thought existed. We arranged to meet soon – and just in time. The man I had dubbed Gustav came looking for his Tadzio. (Gustav's real name was Fritz, perish the thought.)

Our subsequent meeting took place a couple of days later in an old country inn near Munich. The inn had a large beer garden, scented with honeysuckle and jasmine, and the branches of a huge chestnut tree almost touched the ground. Now and then, when the wind stirred, a glimpse of the new moon flickered through the thicket. Somehow, we hardly moved to the subject we initially wanted to talk about. For the second time in my life, I was at peace with myself, and so happy it almost hurt. Here was a potential friend and companion with almost the same background, with whom it was very pleasant to spend an evening.

Careful, Sebastian! Do you know what you are letting yourself in for? Of course I didn't. I just felt close to him on that beautiful summer's evening of 1965.

We discovered that fateful evening that we had much more in common – even that, as young children, our lives crossed unknowingly at the end of World War II, which finally found their culmination, when we were grown up and our paths crossed again.

Frederic was born in Bohemia to a gifted mother, and had two siblings. They were caught unawares in a forced repatriation of the German-Austrian ethnic minority from Czechoslovakia to the Third Reich, or what was left of it. Their cattle train went west and finally stopped at the end of the line in a very picturesque village in Bavaria.

As I mentioned earlier, I was also born in Eastern Europe, in a Hungarian autonomous enclave of Serbia called the Vojvodina with its capital known as Újvidék in Hungarian, Novi Sad in Serbo-Croat and Neusatz in German, on the shores of the mighty river Danube. Újvidék was once part of Hungary and under the rule of the Hungarian crown and Empress Maria Theresia, who ruled from 1740 to 1780, was not only the Empress of Austria, but also the Queen of Hungary; she and her successors expanded and consolidated the Austro-Hungarian empire through dynastic marriages and diplomacy. This establishment of the empire led to internal migration within the Habsburg lands and a feeling of belonging among the various territories. Among other projects, Maria Theresia had the marshes drained along the river Danube and made into arable land. Apart from the local population, she called on the German Swabians, who emigrated to the area and were known as "Danube Swabians". These nations lived in peace with each other until the Great War, and the Vojvodina became known as the bread basket of the Hapsburg Empire. Later on until World War II it traded with its neighbours and remained a prosperous, but politically dormant province of the former Austro-Hungarian Empire. The circumstances surrounding Mother's life were never fully clear to me; for all the questions I asked, I never got satisfactory answers. She remained an enigma. The only reason she gave for our flight was that the Vojvodina had been reclaimed by the Hungarians during World War II, but reverted to Serbia near the end of the war, after which Újvidék took Novi Sad as its official name. I was born during these territorial struggles, which ultimately made me stateless in a hostile, foreign land. Moreover, Mother had married a man with a German surname, making it wise for us all to leave. But how come she had another child when she claimed never having loved her husband? Well who am I, with my "Romany" love life, to criticize "Madonna"?

Frederic and I discovered that, in 1944, my family had camped in a makeshift shelter in a meadow behind his place of birth in Wallern, Bohemia (now called Volary in the Czech Republic). Looking out at this shelter, he recalled that his mother had often said, "I feel very sad for these people without proper clothing for the approaching winter, in a leaky tent and with hardly anything to eat." But comfort was not theirs to give, since they also often went hungry.

Other aspects of my circumstances were much more complicated and difficult. My mother, a farmer's daughter, had attended a Catholic finishing school and was destined for an arranged marriage – not only for her looks, but also for her dowry. The big problem was me.

Mother had a Hungarian childhood sweetheart from Budapest, but was forced into a loveless marriage to a man of German origin. He did not have to go to war, but he volunteered to serve the German nation. Years later, when he tried to emigrate with the family to California, we learned that he had been attached to the SS and had spied for the Germans in Yugoslavia. The French and the other Allies were wary of further trials after Nuremberg and let him go, since there was not sufficient evidence about his activities during the war years.

My misfortune was that I was born in 1942, when my mother's husband was in active service, heaven knows where. He had not seen my mother for over a year. My real father was shot in Újvidék, possibly on my stepfather's orders, but these were only rumours.

When he and my mother got together again near the end of the war, then, he had two sons – one born in 1939, whom he knew about, and one born in 1942, whom he pretended not to know. Our family were pushed from our home to the camp in Wallern (Volary, Frederic's birthplace), via endless train shuttles to Austria. During this time, my half-sister was born, and we did not make it farther west.

There was a lot of friction within the family, and I was branded the scapegoat for all the wrongdoings that incurred his wrath. I still wear the mental scars due to his brutal beatings and sexual abuse, which now and then surface. I often wondered what fate people like him might have after death. On one occasion my mother thought he would kill me because he would not stop beating me. She tried to intervene, but paid the price in having to have a complete upper denture fitted, since he turned on her and finished what he intended to do to me. When he passed his seventy-fifth birthday, he was admitted to a mental asylum, where he died, forgotten by his family, at the age of eighty-five or thereabout.

My half siblings emigrated to Canada, where my half-brother died a few years off his fiftieth birthday of cancer of the oesophagus, overindulging in drinking and smoking. My half-sister went to live in the Rockies with her husband. She was a teacher in the school of which he was headmaster, and lived a withdrawn life, without friends or foes, quite some miles from the next-door neighbours. Their daughter travelled the globe as an English teacher and seemed to be quite successful. She is now somewhere overseas in a teaching post, after having spent years in a post in Seoul, but her present location is not known to me.

Frederic's father married his mother, even though the man was twenty-eight years older than she was. It was his second marriage. He resorted to mental torture and cruelty, which was just as lethal as the physical punishment my stepfather dealt to me.

Gerald, Frederic's brother, was a fine young man of my own age. He was tolerant, and as long as he lived, he never treated me as anything other than a brother. We were all very afraid when, during the height of the breakup of the Yugoslavian state, he was sent as special UN envoy to Bosnia.

You might well ask what he was doing there. The reason was twofold. First, he spoke Serbo-Croat and its dialects very well. It all began when the border opened with Austria in 1956. Their mother went with her three children to an island in the Kvarner bay of Dalmatia, which from then on became their main holiday destination. Frederic was also fluent in Serbo-Croat and translated about fifteen books into German. One was a book by Ivo Andric, who won the Nobel Prize for literature in 1961.

During his diplomatic career, Gerald spent two three-year stints in Belgrade: as a cultural attaché and then as vice ambassador of the German state. During Gerald's first posting in Yugoslavia, the question of compensation for my mother's land, which was substantial, was still dragging its feet. She was in the middle of suing the Yugoslavian state. Gerald managed to put pressure on some influential Yugoslavs he knew, and the claim – not in total, but quite a substantial amount – went through. Since the farm buildings were built during the Austro-Hungarian Empire, I had to travel several times to Hungary as well to have the claim settled, which it eventually was.

The second reason Gerald was selected as a special envoy to Bosnia was that his English was flawless. He had studied in England, at Leeds University, and met an English girl called Alexandra, whom he married. They had three children. His thesis was on Thomas Hardy, whom I read and reread many times.

One evening, soon after we met, Frederic broke the news that I was to meet his mother. Well, I have to admit, I was scared, nervous, and apprehensive. By that time we had not known each other very long. The boyfriend and his mother? But Frederic would not take no for an answer. He decided the meeting was to be in an inn next to the village church. I had stayed there from time to time; it was right at the entrance of his village. I couldn't remember having so many butterflies in my stomach before, or so much apprehension of the unknown. What if she did not like me, or I did not like her?

But on first sight I warmed to her charming way, all dressed in Loden with a frilly blouse with small red roses. I can no longer remember the exact conversation. All I remember is that she spoke Austro-German with a slight lilt, just like me. She was very concerned that Frederic finished his studies and achieved his doctorate. She said if I supported this goal, she would have no objection to us becoming friends. I wondered what Frederic told her before our meeting, since she was more at ease with me than I dared to expect. She hinted about the old Austro-Hungarian way of life and she had also been told of Frederic's affair with Gustav, who was well into his sixties and whom I had seen the night I met Frederic.

We were in our twenties and displayed no gay habits. Let's say, we were not camp. She was a lady and I was beginning to understand how much she and Frederic were alike. Somewhere it was probably painful to know about Gustav, but she hid her feelings extremely well and seemed to underwrite our friendship. In the end she became my "Ersatz Mutter".

In the meantime, Frederic's father made moves to report him to the police. In 1965 Germany, it was still illegal to have a gay relationship. Every town had a vice squad that would react to any accusation made of an illicit relationship. If you happened to be caught, you could end up in prison; this was why the whole movement had to go underground. It seemed that since Oscar Wilde nothing much had changed. Frederic's mother was afraid that Gustav might drag Frederic down.

My stepfather was not much better. Thank God my mother overheard his conversation with the police on the phone, and gave me a ring to go underground or disappear for a while. He had opened a letter in which I told Mother I had a boyfriend.

In my early friendship with Frederic, the only doubt lay with me – not just because of the threats, but because I felt mentally not ready to commit myself to another person again. Yes, I was in love with Frederic from the moment I saw him.

He called me Mandryka, an allusion to the hero of the Richard Strauss opera *Arabella,* a stranger from an eastern province of the empire. This was a reflection not only of my origins but also of the intensity of feeling between us. What was there to be afraid of? In our hours of intimacy, there was as much love as there was doubt. It frightened me, and I asked myself if it would last.

While I was still lying low, there was a headhunter going round in Munich's hotels, trying to woo white staff to emigrate to South Africa for more money, a life in the sunshine, and good opportunities for making a splendid career. The South African government under the new apartheid laws of Dr Verwoerd were looking for young professionals to boost the number of whites, who were outnumbered by a ratio of one to six.

What did I know about apartheid? Here was an opportunity to go missing for a year, and I grabbed it. I signed on as assistant manager of the Langham hotel in Johannesburg, which had reciprocal arrangements with the Dorchester in London's Park Lane.

I did not want to go, but there was no other option open to us. Frederic had to finish his doctorate, and I could not stay forever underground. We were very sad. The day of my departure loomed heavily over us, and our love became more and more tender. We clung together like Siamese twins, sometimes happy; but the parting was always on our minds.

It was a cold and miserable day when Frederic drove me to the airport. All I remember is his face, full of tears, glued to the window in the lounge overlooking the planes arriving and departing. I nearly turned back. Too late – the boarding had begun. My promise to return within a year, if we still felt the same, seemed a lifetime away. We both knew this year could make or break us, and it almost did.

CHAPTER 3

On the Flight to South Africa

During the long flight to Johannesburg, I relived our first six months together. There was something very special about the memories. I almost felt I had betrayed Frederic in leaving him alone for a year. I dreamed of him …

Being nearly at the end of my training, I had managed to get a week's holiday, and we set off in Frederic's white Beetle – not quite an old banger yet, but nearly. Crossing into Austria near Salzburg, we went past the mountains called Streng Berge, where Anton Bruckner had lived. We recalled the evening when we heard the *Romantische*, Bruckner's fourth symphony, in a concert at the Herkules Saal in Munich.

We stopped at an inn to have something to eat. There was a wedding party going on. Most of the guests were dressed in traditional Austrian wear and dancing round a tall maypole. Between the ladies, there seemed to be a competition going on regarding which one was wearing the most fetching *Dirndl*. The von Trapp family would have enjoyed the event.

From there we proceeded to Melk, the majestic monastery overlooking miles of the Danube river valley. There was a wine tasting going on, and it seemed to be more of a drinking affair than a tasting. The imbibers included some of the jolly monks with their red noses and benign smiles. As this was a high baroque monastery, the rooms were magnificent, a more than splendid example of the style. The library alone was a marvel of the period, and the most splendid room I had come across in a long time.

We crossed the river by a small ferry to Maria Haferl, a place of pilgrimage in the Wachau, the romantic area with grape vines growing up to the tops of the hills at both sides. The foliage was already taking on a pre-autumnal colour. We had dinner at the Richard the Lionheart hotel and restaurant in Dürnstein, where we also stayed the night. I had seldom been so happy.

We left the curtains open. The sun came up the following morning, and the valley was covered in mist. From the end of our beds, we could watch the mist slowly rising, to give us the most beautiful awakening of the Danube valley. We still felt inebriated from the past evening – an evening that could only have taken place between two people who were very happy and at ease with each other.

After breakfast we crossed over the bridge near Krems to visit Göttweig Monastery. This was again splendid: a baroque basilica and a tastefully furnished picture gallery of old masters, which you reached by climbing a resplendent staircase.

Leisurely we continued to my beloved Vienna. It was a dream, from the Hotel Sacher to the Demel bakery and coffee house, where, the saying goes, the ruder the waitresses, the better the pastry. As we entered the town, I thought of my first Mozart opera, *Don Giovanni*, and the duet which particularly touched me, "Là ci darem la mano" "There I'll give you my hand, my life." We had booked the Hotel Urania, which was a dusty brocade-and-velvet affair. Everything you touched released a cloud of smelly vapour. It looked ready for refurbishment. The bed was enormous, and the mattress had a hollow in the middle, into which you were bound to fall just by turning round. The best part was the ceiling frescoes, with cherubs like chubby children with wings.

The hotel was conveniently situated between the Prater and St. Stephen's Cathedral (Stephansdom). You could take the circular tram which ran along "the Ring", get off at any station you liked, and rejoin when you wanted to explore Vienna a station further on. This and the sheer beauty of the palatial private residences, apartment houses and government offices enchanted me once again. This was the place I had lived for a few years after 1944, and I still carry it within me.

It was also the place where most of Frederic's relatives had lived. We visited the Zentralfriedhof, immortalized in the last scene of *The Third Man*, and found a few of his uncles' and aunts' graves. Another foray was a tram ride to the seventh district, where most of his relatives used to live. We visited the time-worn church where his maternal grandparents married. We found a side chapel dedicated to the Virgin and child, and lit candles for each other, promising, whatever might happen, that we would never part until the day one of us died.

In our thirties, when we were making more money, we came back to Vienna, often twice a year, to enjoy the opera, theatre, classical concerts, and one or two of the current exhibitions – not forgetting the splendid food, from simple coffee houses to five-star restaurants,

But first on the agenda came the Prater. I always wanted to ride on the giant wheel again. On the top, you had the most spectacular view of Vienna. Once, right at the top, Frederic presented me with a posy of violets, which made me almost cry.

In all sincerity, I cannot paint us as angels. Other encounters happened now and then. But we were always tolerant of little misdemeanours as long as those did not threaten our union.

The opera house had opened again after being bombed by the Americans almost at the end of the war. Luckily some forward-looking town hall executives had the front of the building and foyer shored up to withstand the bombardment. Unfortunately there was no protection for the rest of the house; about a hundred stage sets and all the costumes went up in flames with the rest of the building. A tiresome quarrel ensued which held up the rebuilding: should the auditorium be rebuilt as open plan, which would create hundreds more seats, or should it be rebuilt exactly as it was originally designed? The conservationists won, and the auditorium was rebuilt as it was originally designed.

The grand re-opening took place on 5 November 1955, after the Austrian signing of the State Treaty at the Castle Belvedere in Vienna by all the Allies. The first performance was Beethoven's *Fidelio* under the baton of Karl Böhm.

We saw *Don Giovanni* at the Volksoper, the home of operas sung in German, just as the Coliseum in London presents operas sung in English. We also saw the Schiller play *Maria Stuart* at the world famous "Burgtheater".

Frederic and I wished these carefree days could be repeated, time and time again. When I fell in love with Maja, it hit me pretty hard. Falling in love with Frederic was unstoppable and far more grown-up than love had been with Maja. Her image was slowly retreating and being replaced by Frederic.

Back in Munich, it took quite some time to settle in to work and the daily routine. But I have to admit we were particularly lucky having our early years subsidised by our mothers. Frederic's translations paid well but my job brought in just a pittance, and the hotel did not allow me to take on any moonlighting jobs.

When I finished my official training, I was allowed to stay in the hotel until I left for South Africa. With a little time on our hands, Frederic took me to the island of Krk in the Kvarner Bay, of Dalmatia. At that time we did not know that the island would play a big part in our future lives.

Today there is a bridge, I am told, from the mainland. In our days there was a more or less unreliable ferry service. If you missed one boat, it could be hours before another one came to take you for the fifteen-minute ride. We arrived late in the evening and made the last crossing. Then the question arose: where to sleep? Frederic drove us up a dry riverbed, which was called a road, to a village where he knew some people. Among them was an old peasant woman running a small farmstead. She willingly let us have her bed and moved into the barn, where she kept her livestock, from chickens to goats.

For the beginning of October, the temperature was unusually mild, and the full moon was nearing. Nothing could have been more romantic than the two of us hidden away, off the beaten track. We went swimming by the light of the moon under a sky full of stars. The crickets seemed to be happy with the weather too and made a lot of noise throughout the night. And the night usually ended up with tender moments.

During the daytime we found a secluded bay, only accessible by one boat to anchor. We really had some fun there. There was an inn nearby and on arrival we ordered lunch, which was usually the catch of the day. It was supposed to be a tourist attraction, since you had a clear view of the picturesque, hilly island of Cres. But it was poorly marketed, which we were grateful for.

A typical lunch was freshly baked bread, Yugoslav smoked ham (just as good as Parma ham), and fish with a generous helping of polenta. The local wine was as sour as vinegar, but that did not deter us from having our bottle at lunchtime. Sometimes we had just a picnic with bread, goats cheese, and beef tomatoes.

Then we dreamed the afternoon away in our secluded enclave, hand in hand. Once or twice we stayed overnight, since the innkeepers owned a small cottage on the other side of our hidden beach. Only recently, looking at photographs of these days, did I realise that this heaven was an unforgettable time and could never be repeated.

One afternoon we had a lazy lunch with a glass of wine or so on the terrace of an old hotel in the imperial Austro-Hungarian style overlooking the bay. All the doors and windows were open, and the curtains played in the late summer wind as fallen leaves blew in. The sea lapped at the terrace walls.

Suddenly we heard someone playing the piano version of the *Romance Larghetto*, the slow movement of Chopin's first piano concerto. We listened as in a dream to the piano at our table outside. It was almost too wonderful to comprehend. The afternoon had turned hazy and the mist started rising from the sea.

When the pianist had finished, Frederic went inside and said hello. The lady turned out to be an old baroness and an acquaintance of his.

I cherished that particular event for a long time. Even today, I can feel the magic of the long-gone afternoon coming alive in me whenever I hear Chopin's music.

The days seemed to get ever shorter. I looked forward with some misgivings to my departure. Frederic wanted to celebrate my twenty-third birthday in advance. He chose the Hungarian restaurant Piroska in Munich. There, the Lakatos Brothers entertained the guests – the same family of gypsy fiddlers who kept my mother's wedding party swinging into the early morning hours in Újvidék in 1937.

This was when my maternal grandfather disgraced himself with his son-in-law to be and the family. The night before the event, he gathered as many friends as he could find, and they emptied a hundred-litre barrel of wine, leaving an awful mess behind. There was a frantic clean-up campaign just in time, before the guests arrived and a new barrel was installed.

At the Piroska, there was a commotion going on. A pageboy in the full regalia of the Four Seasons Hotel held up a tablet with the name Sebastian on it and made his way through the restaurant to present me with a large bunch of red roses. The guests looked baffled and so did I. A second pageboy arrived with an enormous birthday cake. After the commotion had died down, I asked the gypsies in Hungarian to play some of Brahms's Hungarian dances including number five to defuse the situation, as well as offering the dining guest's a slice of my cake. The young Rosenkavalier was surprised, as were the guests, that I spoke Hungarian. When the gypsies had finished, the atmosphere in the restaurant was established once more. A further sign of commitment?

And there the dream ended. I was woken by a stewardess, who told me that we would be landing in about an hour at Johannesburg's Jan Smuts Airport, as it was known in 1965. *My God,* I thought, *what have I done?*

The dream was all I had for the long year I was separated from Frederic.

CHAPTER 4

South Africa

On arrival I began to realize that, for all its sophistication, art and culture simply did not exist in Johannesburg. The Dutch Reformed Church and the Afrikaaner rulers did not allow any alcohol to be served on Sundays and opposed the introduction of television. Even the cinemas, which they called "bioscopes", were closed. This year, reading became once again my best companion, as well as writing long letters to Frederic. Reading newspapers, which were censored, was pointless. Calling overseas was expensive and had to be booked in advance, subject to the availability of a translator for whatever language you were going to use during the call, to listen in to your call on behalf of the State..

However, there were three notable events that I recall. Nana Mouskouri sang for a week at the Kyalami Ranch, to entertain the diners. Marlene Dietrich, who stayed in the Langham penthouse and gave us a run for our money, appeared for five concerts at the newly opened civic hall. Mimi Coertse, the South African soprano, gave an evening performance of opera arias, badly chosen, and received only scant praise and applause.

Whatever had been important in my life had vanished. All I could think of was my farewell with Frederic and the promises we had made to each other time and time again. I kept asking myself why I had withdrawn my hand, my love, and my life from Frederic, "là ci darem la mano".

But my life had not been tenable any longer in Austria or Germany. A conviction of any kind would have marked me forever. Doors to managerial posts would have been shut. It would have been no different for Frederic.

Some years before I arrived in Johannesburg, I had made friends with two South African girls while camping with a school friend at Lake Zurich. We had all reached the lake on our bicycles, which were quite primitive if you compare them to the high-tech versions of today. Upon my arrival in Johannesburg, I rang the girls and was immediately invited to a party of a closed circle of friends. It was clear to me that this was indeed a party for gay men and girls. I still can't understand why I did not spot the girls' relationship when I met them at Lake Zurich. In Johannesburg, some members-only bars had a mixed-sex clientele to satisfy the police, who raided them regularly. Nobody seemed to be worried, so why should I? This was a world quite new to me, and not a particularly desired one, since this kind of life was full of lies and deceit.

Rose, one of the girls I had met in Zurich, lived not far from me in Johannesburg. She was the leader of the gang and had everybody in the group under her charismatic spell. This included smoking "dacha," local marijuana, of which she seemed to have an unending supply. No one could find out where it came from. Sometime later she disclosed to me that her parents had smuggled all their money out to the Isle of Man. For that reason, she always stopped over in Douglas to draw lots of cash from the bank before she went to stay in Europe – "overseas", as it was called. That was the first time I heard the expression.

A more personally significant story happened in the first weeks after my arrival in Johannesburg. Crossing Joubert Park on a fine day, I saw a middle-aged lady tumble and take a heavy fall. I rushed to help her. Thank God she seemed not to have broken anything. I helped her to a bench nearby. She was in shock, and I tried to talk to her quietly. I found the "For whites only" written all over the bench offensive. As if the government, which was over-policed anyway, needed this kind of show of white supremacy.

I asked her what made her fall, and she admitted that she got dizzy spells often. She seemed to be more bruised than anything else. My arm to help her get home was not refused. Yes, she was Afrikaans, as if that mattered to me in any way. She lived in a neat town house not far from the park. When I rang the bell, a young man about my age opened the door. He was her youngest son, Frank.

We got his Mama into the house, and he offered me a cup of coffee. I was grateful for it, since I thought his mother's fall looked very dangerous and I was worried. After serving coffee, he asked me if I was German by any chance, since he recognized my accent. I said yes, Austro-German. He had recently been released from hospital after suffering from depression. He told me that he would like to emigrate to a German-speaking country, which in those days meant taking a return ticket and just not coming back. He would ask for political asylum. He had a pen pal in Germany and he was aiming to settle there.

Years later he turned up in London, out of the blue, and told me that he had settled in Wiesbaden and felt very happy. Mind you, he didn't look it! He felt England and the UK in general was a country he would not like to know. He had the attitude of a hard-bitten Afrikaaner. Poor Frank! And as he appeared, so he vanished, never to be heard of again, by me or, most of all, his parents. In South Africa, we had become good friends and spent a lot of time together; I helped him with his German. Our political views differed to such an extent that we always seemed to end up in quarrels, so we stopped talking politics.

Frank's parents adopted me as if I were their own son; they became my South African parents. Apart from the home in Johannesburg, they also had a farm near Hartbeestport Dam, not far from Johannesburg. The farm was run by a manager. I spent quite a lot of weekends there. When we parted, they promised to come and see me in London if I went to live there, as I had indicated I would once I was settled.

There was another way to my home in Johannesburg, taking the road instead of walking through the park. A lot of coffeehouses flourished along this road, places where backpackers and flower children met. Often one of the boys or girls played the guitar and sang folk songs, which were a bit of home for all English-speaking people, who came from countries as far away as New Zealand and Australia.

I do not know why everything in the past seems to be in one's memory beautiful, and longer lasting. I even had time to do an odd job here and there to make more money for the trip home to Frederic. That was until, about halfway through my stay in South Africa, I met Hendrik.

Hendrik was a good-looking young man from Dutch stock, and I was attracted to him as soon as we met. He was gentle, beautiful, and not available. He pushed about a girl in a wheelchair, since she could not walk due to multiple sclerosis. I saw them when they arrived at a house party. When I inquired with Rose, what had happened to the young man pushing the girl about, she just replied that he had been a wild boy until recently. Then he met the girl and, in a kind of caprice, found his mission to look after her.

Why now? By that time, Frederic and I were halfway through our year of separation. And now this had happened.

Hendrik and I drove out to the Kyalami racetrack for a talk which lasted for many hours. I wanted to see more of him and he wanted me too. All the talking did not make the slightest bit of difference; mutual liking and sex appeal was simply there.

We started a secret affair. We were both aware of what we were doing: Hendrik was betraying his friend and I Frederic. Our naiveté was so strong that he wanted to withdraw from his Florence Nightingale's role for his friend. Somehow I thought it would not work. I often encountered deep regret in his face, and I had a similar feeling.

I told Frederic that, after all, I had to break with him. It was the saddest letter I had ever written. I still can't understand what possessed me to do such a thing. As another good friend asked me, why did you have to do that, could you not just have written about the birds and the bees? The affair with Hendrik would be at an end anyway when I went back overseas. Sound advice, but a little late in the day – the damage was done.

Hendrik was just as lovable as Frederic, but not of the same background, and he did not have the same urge to travel. I tried not to think about it.

No matter how hard we tried, one day the love and sex had gone. The friendship remained. We drove out to the racetrack and talked again for a long while. We came to the conclusion that we were from different worlds. Since the sex had gone, there probably would not be much left, and after a while we would drift apart.

As was typical for me, I thought I was in love with Hendrik. But, having got him when he had refused many other men, all of a sudden I did not feel proud about it. Payback time reared its ugly head. I could either write a grovelling letter to Frederic or find myself engulfed in a new personal problem of my own doing.

As much as I detested myself for having written a farewell letter to Frederic at the time, it took all my mental energy to persuade him this was just a one-off affair which was destined not to last. Having nearly lost Frederic through my own stupidity, I remembered what we had promised each other, and the love came gradually, haltingly back again. And it was going to last for almost half a century, since we both knew that we irrevocably did belong to each other.

One night the clan drove out to a rich boy's house between Johannesburg and Pretoria. We drove along an avenue of jacaranda trees in full bloom, and the evening was heavenly scented. The boy's parents were away. He had been given an ultimatum: to separate from his boyfriend, or they would throw him out of the house on their return. We were all under the influence of drugs and drinks, and what happened that evening was a tragedy.

Someone said very loudly, almost screaming, "But they are dead!" We all rushed to the swimming pool and saw two bodies floating. The rich boy and his boyfriend were dead. None of us knew that they had made a pact – rather than be separated, they would commit suicide.

"Let us call the emergency services and get the hell out of here as quickly as we can," Rose said. We grabbed our belongings and vanished from the scene not one moment too early, since the sirens could be heard a few miles off. None of us wanted to get involved. We took a longer route home, since the authorities surely had planted roadside blocks.

One night, a good time later, I had a call from Juta, a girl who went with me to South Africa and had also worked at the same hotel in Munich. She had introduced me to the naughty Boccaccio's *Decameron*. She now worked at the Kyalami Ranch hotel near the racetrack. I asked Hendrik if he could take me there in the next few days to see her again.

This was at the time that Nana Mouskouri was entertaining the diners in the evenings. From the staff quarters, we had quite a good view of the stage and stayed to the end of the evening. Sadly, Juta was later caught on a drug run out of Johannesburg, and I never heard from her again. Goodness knows how many years she had to spend in jail. Sentencing depended on the amount she carried, but was never less than ten years.

Meantime, I had written to Frederic and simply put my life into his hands. I admitted that I had been very much in the wrong. Nothing happened for a while. Then I received a postcard from Munich, the cafe Glockenspiel. The card arrived with only one word on it: *Szeretlek*. In Hungarian, that means "I love you". I could hardly believe that he had forgiven me. I have the postcard to this day.

Now that Frederic was back in my life, his Gustav and my Hendrik had to go. We were looking forward to our reunion once again.

After less than one year, I was offered a promotion to manager understudy for a smaller hotel in Durban, with the view to taking over the running of it in the very near future. I could not disclose at this stage that I planned to leave. I asked to think about it on a long overdue holiday.

Frank and his parents took me to the train station in Johannesburg. The whistle blew and the train started its slow descent towards Durban, down the very picturesque Drakensberg Mountains. There I had a week's holiday and travelled on to Lourenço Marques, in Mozambique, in an old Fokker Friendship.

From the moment I arrived, I had the feeling of coming home to Frederic. The town was a jewel of colonial dimensions, without apartheid. The jacarandas here were as beguiling as they were on the way to Pretoria. It was a reminder that blacks and whites could live in harmony, but it was too late for South Africa. The air was fragrant throughout the town, from the jacarandas, lilies, frangipani, and lots of bougainvillea, all adding their colours in a rainbow fashion. Port Elizabeth may have been the garden city of South Africa, but Lourenço Marques was the garden city of southern Africa.

I spent another week in Lourenço Marques at a hotel on the cliffs, facing the endless Indian Ocean. One reached the sea over a narrow strip of stairs hewn into the rocks, and had the beach all to oneself. It was indeed a subtropical paradise, full of flowers swaying in the gentle breeze off the Indian Ocean.

And suddenly the day arrived to start the long way back to Europe and Frederic.

CHAPTER 5

Amsterdam and the Homecoming

There was no such thing as a supersonic plane in the 1960s, and even jets were not common. You had to make do with a turbo airliner, which had to be refuelled often. We flew first to Dar es Salaam, then to Nairobi. We made yet another stop in Benghazi before embarking on the last leg of the journey to Amsterdam.

Finally the plane taxied its way to the arrivals hall at Schiphol. There were no movable gangways attached to the airport building in the 1960s. The plane, a Lockheed Super Constellation, had become quite familiar to me, since I had spent a day, a night, and more on it on the way to Frederic.

I looked up and saw a smiling face. Our reunion can't be described. We both had matured enormously during the year we were apart. Each of us had played the field and understood fully what it meant to have a happy relationship. The love between Frederic and Mandryka started all over again, just as it had a distant year ago. We did not need any words or explanations, and our hands did not like to part in saying hello. We were like Mandryka and Arabella in Strauss's opera.

All Frederic could say was that we would never again be apart for such a long time, and this was true to the end of our relationship.

Frederic, having arrived in Amsterdam a few days prior to my arrival, managed to get tickets for the Concertgebouw, where interludes and overtures by Richard Wagner were being performed. Afterwards we had a fantastic dinner at one of the fashionable restaurants in town. Needless to say, the next day I was hung over from the long flight and the amount of wine we had drunk with dinner, and decided to stay in bed all day. But the following day we felt fit to visit the Rijksmuseum, the Stedelijk, and the Rembrandthuis.

From Amsterdam we took two leisurely days to drive to Bavaria, where we stayed but a short time. Thereafter we drove to the island in the Kvarner Bay for a week or two.

During the year I was away, Frederic had been to Újvidék to participate in a meeting of the Yugoslav writers' union. The town had taken on a different look, since the Serbian authorities had started to bulldoze the old buildings. Among the buildings still standing were my parents' house and a few others. More and more Serbians had also emigrated into the town to undermine the autonomy of the state of the Vojvodina.

We crossed the border with Hungary next to Szeged, Grandmother's hometown, with a stop in Tokay, then on to Budapest.

The Hungarians lived well, loved parties and generally had a good time. Communism was only felt in not being able to buy Western goods. It also did not allow citizens to travel beyond its borders, unless you were an active member of the Communist Party and they could be sure you would return. Among other irritants, investment in building and infrastructure was non-existent; many buildings were left damaged as they had been after the war.

I was quite happy to visit Budapest, the city of my father's, maybe finding relatives. The family name of Bartók is quite distinguished and was fairly in evidence at the cemetery, but alas, the search was not successful.

We were under the patronage of a charming lady we knew from the island in Croatia. She got us a hotel at a much discounted price, as well as tickets for the Hungarian State Opera, which performed *Lohengrin* and *Simon Boccanegra* while we were in Budapest. Both operas were sung in Hungarian, which sounded quite funny to Frederic and me. And poor old Elsa von Brabant was about twenty years older than Lohengrin.

We also enjoyed the good food. Wherever we went, we did not see too many signs of communism. The most obvious indications were the war damage, such as holes from the impact of ammunition having hit the houses, mostly in the failed uprising of 1956 and general symptoms of neglect. Budapest looked ready for the phoenix to rise from the ashes. The only problem was me again. I was shadowed by the police almost everywhere we went. This was because, when I filled in the visa form on the border, I had to give my mother's maiden name, which was very Hungarian.

On our return to Germany, Frederic put me up with friends in Munich. After a few days I had to tell him I could not stay any longer, since they were trying to have it off with me. To them I seemed to be easy game. Frederic was appalled and we left for his home village, where he put me up in an out-of-the-way inn.

We tried to stay out of trouble. A few days later, as I was coming down the main road of the village with Frederic and his mother, we bumped into his father, who attacked all three of us with choice language. If ever I have seen a volcano break out, it was his mother. She was a charming lady who had begun to despise her much older husband. I never saw her as angry again as she was on this occasion.

What now? A dear lady friend of Frederic's and his mother's gave me an annex of her house in which to endure what might be called a house arrest. She looked after me very kindly.

It was time we made a move. We departed within a week or two to Yugoslavia.

Frederic had to teach for a year in Thessaloniki before he could join me at my next destination: England. This was the decision of the German Academic Exchange, which promised him a visiting lecturer's post in Cambridge where he was to write his second doctorate and tutor in German for a small emolument, on a part-time basis. I spent the year odd-jobbing in London hotels. After Thessaloniki, Frederic kept me company there. Then we had more security and knew where we were going to go.

But before Frederic went to Thessaloniki, we had the summer together. On our way through Yugoslavia for another sojourn on the island, we were stopped twice by the military and police. Of course my passport had to have the new post-war name of my place of birth, and none of them could understand why I did not speak Serbian. This happened time and time again and I almost got paranoid, until the intelligence service finally established that I was the stepson of a man who had spied for the Germans, way back in the late thirties and early forties.

Nothing happened to me, but I was twice hauled into Zagreb's police station and interrogated. When my fool of a stepfather went on holiday to Istria sometime in the early 1970s, he just escaped arrest by a couple of hours, fleeing to Italy. Had more modern communication existed, he probably would have landed in the nick.

On the island, Frederic found a place we both fell in love with. We went to a solicitor to buy the primitive peasant cottage, without running water or electricity. Frederic knew a local couple who had a small farmstead in the village, and the farmer came with us to sign the contract, since foreigners couldn't buy property in communist Yugoslavia. The contract was technically a kind of lease, which we entered into on Frederic's mother's behalf. The man was paid for his services and also for the repairs which accrued during the winters. We used the cottage for years before it had to be given back when the state of Yugoslavia fell apart.

Visiting the lawyer was like going back to Dickensian times. All his files and documents were handwritten. Stacks of papers were piled from floor to ceiling on three sides of his office. He had a stand-up writing desk with a desk lamp, a small and narrow window which gave him just enough light to write the contract with, an ink feather, and arm protectors. Now and then he looked above his half-glasses to see if Frederic and the Yugoslav friend could follow his mumbling. It took the best part of a morning until the documents were completed and duly signed by all parties.

In this cottage, the two of us would build many fond memories. We had the whole summer in front of us, and we made the most of it. And there we could mind our own business unhindered. I typed Frederic's first dissertation on my little travel typewriter and helped him with two translations from Serbo-Croat into German. He more or less dictated to me as we went along.

Gustav was forgotten. Much later in our life together, I found some pictures from Mykonos, where he and Frederic had spent a holiday together while I was away in South Africa. But by the time I came back to Europe, the affair was over. Gustav was a senior editor of a well-known publishing house, and it was he who had given Frederic most of the translation work.

On a couple of occasions, Frederic had to go home. I drove him to Ljubljana to catch the fast train from Belgrade to Salzburg, which ran every day, terminating in Munich. I was always glad to pick him up when he returned.

Slowly we made the cottage habitable. We added blue gingham curtains, surrounds for the huge fireplace, and scatter cushions on chairs and benches. This brightened up the kitchen cum living room no end. Some low chairs made of wood and covered with sea grass enabled us, on cooler days, to sit on the slightly elevated hearth in a semicircle. There was usually a goulash in the pot, sizzling away. With the local peasant bread and a seasonal bowl of tomato salad, the meal took no time to prepare and even less to eat. The glow of ship lamps gave the place a very romantic feel. We had a local carpenter to make a wooden privy. On the sloping roof of the house, he made a fixture to hold a large canister. When filled with refreshing, cool water from our own well, the canister provided us with an enjoyable daily shower.

The landmark of the cottage was a very tall and handsome cypress. The small terrace had a well and faced west. We often used it for a barbecue for ourselves or for friends joining us for a social evening. Nobody would have guessed how happy we were; we kept our feelings inside when we were in front of friends and family. We enjoyed the cottage – hauling up water from the well, making do with ship's lamps instead of electricity. Even though it was quite some time ago, I can still hear the cicadas chirping there.

I think the tranquillity of the cottage and its surroundings were the reason why we spent so many months on our own, which not only made us partners, but also gave us enough time to mature for a life together.

Of course there was the usual horseplay which often ended up in sex. We tried our hands on do-it-yourself projects which often fell apart, and we simply erupted in laughter.

We also read a lot. One day I asked Frederic about an article, "Wie bei Dostojewsky" by Herbert Eisenreich. I read it in a literary supplement, and it impressed me. I wanted to know whether he was a notable writer. At that point, Frederic started reading it. His opinion was that Eisenreich was better than average, but still a literary lightweight. But he did not want to discount him entirely, since Eisenreich was also a member of the Yugoslav writers' union.

There came another sunny and beautiful day. Frederic got our first beer of the day from the bottom of the well, where he had stored it earlier that day in a bucket, getting it up with the help of a wheel and chain. Suddenly a gentleman appeared on the path in front of the cottage. The path was hemmed in on either side by stone walls about five feet high, and his head was just visible over the top. I looked up and he announced himself as Herbert Eisenreich. "I found out that you are spending the summer here, and since I was on my way home from Belgrade to Vienna, I thought to pay you a visit."

A villager had pointed out our cypress to him. That was how his head and that of his wife, Bumby, a fellow Hungarian, appeared in our front garden. "We are just dropping in for coffee and will be on our way to Vienna," he told us. They stayed for three days of indulgence and debauchery, filled with drink and food. One night when we still felt hungry, Bumby and I went out and cut some twigs, on which we fried sausages over the open fire.

It was strange that our unusual visitors should suddenly appear to visit Frederic just a few days after we read Eisenreich's article. And yet in another way it was not surprising. Even Jara Ribnikar, who was a writer and the secretary of the writers' union, knew of Frederic's affair, but never mentioned a word of objection because we were such close friends. Frederic phoned her from time to time. One time we were completely broke, and Frederic jokingly said, "We are gathering blackberries to survive." She immediately sent us a postal order to help us with our cash flow problem.

Unfortunately the day came to leave our paradise and face reality again. We made the house safe for the winter and packed our belongings. When we left, we joined hands, looked at the cypress, and made a wish to come back again.

It was early September when we set off for Thessaloniki. The landscape along the coastal road was simply breathtaking. The mountains remained with us right up to the end of the road; many of the more distant ones were already snow-capped. We turned inland into a flat valley, which then was part of Yugoslavian Macedonia and is still disputed today: does it belong to Serbia or to Greece? We headed towards Lake Ochrid, secluded and surrounded by mountains and dense forest towards Albania.

There was only one car in front of our hotel. The car had a hand-painted number plate, and Frederic was told it belonged to the Cuban ambassador to Albania. Yugoslav folksongs were coming out of the dining room, which had only one table, occupied by the ambassador, his chauffeur, and two security guards. The very young singer giving a rendition of gypsy songs was Esma Redzepova, with a band. We found out that, whenever the Cubans felt like a good meal and female company, they headed over the mountains to the hotel on the shores of the lake.

It was one of our biggest surprises when, in 2010, Esma Redzepova appeared at the Royal Festival Hall in London. Many exiled Yugoslavs and people like Frederic and me, for one reason or other, turned up and made the evening into a huge success. Almost everybody got up, swinging in the aisles and getting into the feel of the evening.

Since she could not have children of her own, Esma fostered about forty-five boys and girls during her career, giving them a home and a proper education. Thank you, Esma! She later appeared in the Eurovision song contest in Malmö in 2013.

In Ochrid, Sweti Naum was a decommissioned orthodox chapel across the lake from our hotel. It had been a lookout for marauders in the middle ages. Now it was our lookout, me with my arm around Frederic's shoulder, watching the fog lifting and the sun coming through. It was another sign by which we understood that our friendship was blessed.

All too soon we left Macedonia and entered Greece. Thessaloniki was Frederic's posting for a year. A contact gave us a key and sent us to a suburb called Harilau, where a bungalow was waiting for us. The last incumbent had put all the furniture in storage, which we had to release to furnish the house and kitchen. Having done that, it looked quite homey. Luckily we had brought our air mattresses and sleeping bags with us, since the nights were getting chilly.

We amassed quite a few friends in the first months when I was there to help Frederic to settle in. Beautiful Niki, who was working for the Goethe Institute, had a lot of admirers and friends and did not mind when Frederic and I helped lessen her burden. Greek gays are very different from those in the rest of Europe; they manage to become lovers and friends at the same time.

On one of my last evenings there, we gave a farewell party. We put some records by Mikis Theodorakis on the turntable and ended up with the military invading our premises. Under military rule, Theodorakis was banned, since he had written a few songs the military found unacceptable. He had overstepped the line in criticising them. They confiscated our records, gave Frederic and me a warning, and asked all our Greek friends to appear at the police station the following day.

After Frederic's first trimester, we had to part. We travelled from Thessaloniki through Yugoslavia, and Frederic left the train in Salzburg. I continued to Munich and changed trains to Ostend, where I had to board a ship to Dover and immigration. I was quite apprehensive about whether I would be able to pass through immigration unhindered, since my letter of sponsor ship was almost a year old, which I had on me from the respected member of the Bar I met in South Africa. The officer told me, "when you arrive in London, please ask your sponsor for another letter and go to see an officer at the home office to allow you to stay in the United Kingdom", was all he said. After all Christmas was just round the corner and it was bitterly cold.

CHAPTER 6

The Cambridge Years

Frederic came to London in the late 1960s. And as the German Academic Exchange promised, he was appointed lector, a junior lecturer in Cambridge. He had to write a new dissertation in English, which meant he had to master writing as well as speaking a new language. He had been a classical scholar and had not learned any modern languages, apart from basic French and English, before his fourth year of high school. His degree was eventually handed to him at the Senate House in Cambridge, which he accepted wearing a traditional hat and gown. His mentor was none other than his professor, who after two years took him under his wing once again at a prestigious university in London.

In the meantime, I was moving around in one or another capacity to quite a few London hotels. For a while I settled in a smallish hotel overlooking Kensington Gardens, which was a home away from home for prominent opera stars such as Elisabeth Schwarzkopf and dignitaries such as Billy Graham, the Bible basher. If you ask me, the weirdest thing that happened at the hotel was Billy Graham's henchmen counting tin buckets of money donated by the public – counting it in the middle of the hotel's lounge while Billy Graham kept watch. What a greedy, suspicious sod he had become, and all in the name of our Lord.

I had the job of assistant manager. There was a pretty girl, Brenda, in reception, a sweet and lovely girl from Ireland. I soon began an affair with her. Yes, another one! One day she told me that her family would emigrate to America soon, and why didn't I join them? To begin with, I did not know what kind of life would be there for us – probably as orange pickers. No, thank you.

Frederic found out what was going on and had a go at me. "I can fight another man but not a woman. You must do as you see fit." He rescued me from another folly. What was the matter with me? But again our union held, and we returned to being the loving friends all our friends knew. But what did they really know? Our utmost tenderness was private; we never talked about it to friends or family.

Frederic and I fell into the swinging London scene. This was a great time to be in a country with absolute freedom. Everything was happening. Great Britain having recently decriminalised homosexuality between consenting adults over 21 years of age in private, we went and bought two black capes with red linings in Carnaby Street and caused quite a stir wherever we went. It was also the time of avant garde cinema and films like *Teorema* (Theorem), *If*, and *A Clockwork Orange*.

I imagine Frederic had his time in Cambridge too, and was no angel, but it was only within a circle of like-minded people and didn't go any further. In a different way he was as good-looking as myself, which went down well in male-oriented Cambridge.

After breaking up with Brenda, I left that hotel and applied to another, again to work as an assistant manager. From the letter inviting me to an interview, I could not work out if the manager was a man or a woman. It just said "Manager, G. Langer". I announced myself at reception, and they asked me to sit down the manager would not be long. It was hard to believe but a young lady approached me. She was the female- manager and very pretty too. She gave her name, and before I could come up with mine, I got up and fell over an ashtray placed next to my chair. It was one of these abominable stand-up affairs. "Well, you have had it now," I thought, but far from it. I got the job there and then, sealed with a drink at the bar and lunch in the restaurant. She could not have had that many interviews, but she gave me the position. She attributed it to female intuition.

I frequently went to Cambridge over weekends, when Frederic had no commitments on. Often we missed the hour of curfew and had to climb the back gates of his college, which were about ten or twelve feet high.

Thank God we never came to any harm or ripped our clothing, like the characters in Tom Sharpe's novel *Porterhouse Blue.*

I learned that Frederic was having an affair with a good-looking student. I could see very little wrong in it, since his friend also had a steady boyfriend. Until the weekend we were invited by Frederic's friend to a town in the shires, where all the trouble began.

Frederic's friend's boyfriend made a pass at me, or maybe it was the other way round. It was obvious we fancied each other. He nodded toward the door, and I followed in about five minutes. He was already undressed in a bedroom nearby and had left the door open. It took me no time to get undressed as well, and we landed in bed together.

Frederic must have noticed what was going on, and followed me in a short while. There we were, cuddling naked on the bed. Frederic had one of his rare outbursts of temper, announcing, "We are going straight home. I will pack and move out."

"Okay," I said. "As you wish."

Not another word was spoken till we got to our home and he started to pack. When his anger settled down a little, I asked him if he wanted some coffee, and perhaps a brandy, before he left. He just broke down and cried.

After all, he was not an innocent party in the dilemma he got us into. This time it was for me to ask him to sleep on it. If he felt the same way in the morning, he could go on his way.

Sometime in the middle of the night, I sensed somebody coming into my room. The duvet moved, and a body pushed close to mine. I discovered in the morning that he had finished the brandy and was probably drunk before he came to bed. I let him sleep till early afternoon, since I could not wake him. Another cliff was circumnavigated, and we carried on with our lives as if nothing had happened. He went back to Cambridge and I to work.

Almost from the beginning, I experienced a tension with the female-manager I was working for. She had taken a shine to me and, as it turned out later, had fallen in love with me in a big way. I liked her because she was really pretty. It took no time at all for us to begin an affair. She also made it her business to find out who the "Frederic" was who kept ringing me. All calls in the 1960s had to go through a switchboard situated in the reception, where all could hear.

Frederic knew about the affair, but did not question me closely. When he casually mentioned it, I told him that it was my fault as well, and who knew if it would last. I was already beginning to be annoyed about her possessiveness.

We entered the summer, which, apart from my two-week holidays, Frederic spent with his mother and friends in Bavaria. From then on, we used public phones, since we did not want to go through the switchboard or Frederic's landline, as this again was in the hallway for everybody to hear.

During a trip to the Isle of Wight, my manager/lover dropped a bombshell: didn't I think it was time we announced our engagement and got married? She wanted a family and time was running out for her, since she was quite a bit older than myself. She was not kidding, oh no. She was dead serious about it.

This was definitely a nonstarter for me. I walked out of my job and out of her life, something I had never done before.

This was about the time when Frederic and I were packing to move to our first London property together. It was against Frederic's wishes, since he wanted to wait until his tenure with the university was confirmed. My argument was, first, that house prices could only go up; second, in the area we wanted to live, the rents were more than a mortgage payment on a two-bedroom flat; and three, we could always sell if by any chance the London lecturer's job did not materialize. It was also beneficial for me, since my living situation usually went with my job. I cherished the idea that we had a joint property, and should anything go wrong, I could live permanently in our own place. Frederic's tenure was granted a week later.

The flat was on the ground floor, with its own entrance. On the first floor, there was another flat with its own entrance, and a staircase to the first floor. The building was at the end of a terraced street.

CHAPTER 7

The London Years and Beyond

It was November 1968 when we first temporarily moved to London. A friend of mine in Johannesburg had given me the advice to go to Kangaroo Corner at Earls Court, where Aussies, Kiwis, and Springboks met each other or just picked up their mail. They were mostly on two-year travel and work permits, a scheme which still exists. But the seedy atmosphere and exorbitant rents have since driven the dwindling numbers further west, mostly working as bar staff or nannies. Gone are the landlords' listings of "No Wogs or Irish" on the board just outside the tube station. How times have changed!

Our arrival was fairly late in the evening. We stayed in a cheap hotel called Hammonds, near Victoria Station, for a guinea a night with a cooked breakfast of sorts. Frederic got very homesick, and there was nothing I could do other than to talk to him soothingly. Sometimes the sex helped, since these tender moments made his new life and mine more tolerable. I also took him along to most of my interviews. He would wait for me in a Lyons Corner House nearby, where the coffee always tasted of onions.

The contact I had in London was a respected member of the Bar. He happened to be in South Africa on a business trip during the time I worked there. There was the suggestion of "a casting couch". I was fed up with this business. Why should I sleep with somebody who arranged a few of my interviews and treated me like a rent boy? I just walked out on him and began my own search to get a work permit to stay in London.

This was granted for a year. Thereafter I had to go to the Aliens Registration Bureau in Conduit Street to get a further year granted, and so did Frederic. We joked that it felt like having a role in *Star Trek*, being beamed up to the Aliens Registration Bureau.

In the meantime, Frederic's homesickness got so bad that we had a real struggle. It was hard to get him over the parting from his family, in particular from his beloved mama. He cried and cried, but there was not a damn thing I could or would do about it. One evening it got so bad that in all the confusion to get home, I left my briefcase with all my documents, passport, and references in a phone booth outside Green Park tube station. I only realized what I had done when the train pulled into Earls Court.

What now? A quick response was needed. I hailed down the next black cab and directed the driver to Green Park. I think I almost died a thousand deaths of fear. Losing my passport, which could render me stateless for the fourth time in my life. I jumped out at the station with the cabbie in hot pursuit. Lo and behold, there was the neglected briefcase smiling at me from the telephone booth. After explaining the perilous state I had been in, I managed to mollify the cabbie. I wanted to give him all the money I had on me, but he would have none of it, and the matter was settled.

I took the next train to Earls Court and made my way back to our basement bedsit, happy to be greeted by Frederic. I was so relieved that the incident could be glossed over that I decided to tell him about it when he felt a little better.

Often in those days we tossed a coin to decide whether we should go out to the pub to have a couple of beers, or feed the ever-so-greedy, tampered-with gas and electric meters. That evening we stayed at home and spent hours locked together to release the tension.

Slowly Frederic got over his homesickness, and we could begin to explore what was on in London. We went regularly to a concert or the opera. There were usually cheap seats available if you were prepared to sit in the gods at Covent Garden or a back balcony seat at the Royal Festival Hall. The price tag ranged from a florin up to seven shillings and sixpence, which we could just about afford.

These outings gave Frederic and me a new lease of life. We enjoyed the farewell *liederabend* of Elisabeth Schwarzkopf at the Royal Festival Hall, with lieder mainly by Schubert, as well as Mahler's "Kindertotenlieder" and the famous "Four Last Songs" by Richard Strauss. Schwarzkopf was still a very handsome woman in those days, and the perfect artist.

Ilse Wolf was another German-born artist who had to leave Hitler's Germany in 1939. We went to many of her *liederabende*. One of her signature songs was "The Shepherd on the Rock" by Schubert. She performed it throughout the kingdom, and we became very fond of her.

The Halle often performed under the baton of Sir John Barbirolli. Sir Adrian Boult also conducted various orchestras in the UK after the BBC had pensioned him off in his fifties. It was widely accepted that he made the London Philharmonic Orchestra great again. He beckoned us back to the Royal Festival Hall many times with a wide range of composers and his own style of interpretation and conducting.

It was also the time of the music pubs, with live bands performing in almost every district of the capital. We went to a different one also fairly regularly. We learned to know the East End very well, just as well as the posh districts. You could go to Hampstead during the summer evenings, to Kenwood House Gardens, and listen to a splendid orchestra and famous conductors. A seat on the grass was half a crown.

For a while I had time on my hands because I was switching jobs, and we went for a week to Hammamet, Tunisia. We had beautiful weather from sunrise to sunset, every day. We also took long walks on the endless sandy beach. It was the olive harvest time, and the natives invited us to join them and have bread, cheese, and of course olives.

One day in late autumn, Frederic asked bashfully whether it would be all right by me if he went home to Bavaria for Christmas. He promised to be back for the New Year. Well, I had no problem with Frederic wanting to go home to Bavaria. I took a temporary job in a hotel, to look after twenty or thirty dowager matrons of the worst kind from Christmas evening to the morning after Boxing Day. Some hotels made such deals to help the once beautiful and still rich to get over a lonely Christmas. This was common in the fifties and sixties, since it was an easy way to get Mama out of sight so she would not spoil her family's good time.

It was quite an experience. It included about five meals a day. On the second day they had already started to argue among each other. What typified the situation was the boredom they experienced between meal times. I overheard one of the "ladies" complaining to her friend that she would not give up the heavy cream tea, since it had been paid for and she wanted her money's worth. I kept well out of their way. Barbara Cartland, come back – all is forgiven!

On December 31, Frederic and I went up to Trafalgar Square, along with tens of thousands of revellers, to hear Big Ben strike midnight and to celebrate New Year's Eve with a glass of champagne from the duty-free shop, compliments of Frederic's Mama.

Shortly after the New Year, my headhunter's office rang me and said there was another assistant manager's job going at a private club, if I would be interested? Of course I was interested and got an invitation for an interview. Not long after, I accepted their job offer. At last I had a foot in the door, working for the English establishment – a private club.

About one year on, the chairman had dinner with his lady wife at the club and asked if l would be free to have dinner with him the following evening. He indicated there was a third party involved, and I would be put in the picture the following day.

I wondered what it was all about. It could not be the push from my job, so it must be something interesting. I could hardly wait.

The third man at our dinner was a long-standing friend of our chairman. He was in charge of a gentlemen's club, which was looking for a replacement for its retiring manager. The dinner went well, but I felt watched by both sides.

The secretary of the gentlemen's club later gave me a ring and invited me for another dinner with the chairman. This was when I got to know the club's deputy chairman, who would become my mentor, and a few members of the committee. The first question they asked was whether I had taken on British citizenship. This I could easily answer: some mornings before, I had had a letter from the Home Office that the swearing of the oath of allegiance would take place in about a fortnight's time at my district court of law. There was no question about my competence or doubt in my ability to run the club. But my age – and underage looks – gave reasonable doubt whether the members would accept me. There again, I thought I caught the whiff of the casting couch. Surely not?

I felt much disappointment when I got a letter telling me that my association with the club would not materialize. During the next few months, I kept looking around, under the assumption that something would turn up sometime.

One day before I left for work, a letter with a familiar coat of arms landed on my doormat. The club had sent an apology to me. The older candidate they had selected for the manager's position had messed up his trial period, and they were looking for a manager again. They invited me to reconsider the position.

What did I have to lose? I just wanted my accommodation upgraded from a bedsit to a self-contained flat, and a rise after a successful trial period. My terms were discussed by the committee, and twenty-three of the twenty-four welcomed my appointment. I attributed my success in part to the very involved chairman at my first club, who liked the way I tackled problems at work. He recommended me. It was his judgement that I was capable of being more than an assistant.

When I was established, I invited my South African mum and dad to come to London. I had kept in touch with all those years. In the meantime, they had sold their farm as well as their town house and lived in Pietermaritzburg.

They embarked on the long trip to see me one more time. I showed them as much of London and its history as my time allowed. I also took them to the Haymarket Theatre to see *Lady Windermere's Fan* with Googie Withers, the very camp Australian actress. We also went to the Coliseum, where the English National Opera offered a very good production of *La Traviata*. Mum was overwhelmed, since she and Dad had never been to an opera house before, let alone gone overseas.

They were such a nice couple. I will never forget them, since they had looked after me at a time when I was very homesick, giving me their love and care in a foreign land. It was not very long after their visit that both of them died, and I felt grateful that they had made the effort to see me one more time.

PART II

Frederic and I

Great Travel Stories
and Interludes

CHAPTER 8

Egypt, When the World Was Ours

In the 1970s, it became apparent that Frederic's mother could no longer manage her life alone in a Bavarian mountain village. Moreover, since she originally came from Vienna, she never got used to the rural life and yearned for a big city. So she came to live with us in London and rarely went back to the Bavarian mountains.

Luckily the owners of the maisonette on the first floor of our building moved out. They gave us first refusal, as they had promised during the time they lived upstairs. We had become good friends. They were Singhalese, a loveable pair. Their astrologer, whom they hired to look into their childless marriage, advised them to move house, asserting the lady would not be able to conceive any children in their present home. He suggested finding a safe house, and they moved to Ruislip. They even brought their front door with them, since the Ceylonese believed that this would keep bad spirits at bay. Needless to add, they will soon celebrate their golden anniversary, and they never had any offspring.

Frederic's mother moved in upstairs, which turned out to be the best solution all round. The language was no problem. When I met Frederic and she realized that we would probably settle in London, she started to read English novels. She understood English – sometimes only too well – but in front of both of us, she was a bit shy, since she was never sure whether we would correct her or laugh at her mistakes. As if we would have dared.

Unfortunately, this put additional pressure on our financial situation. We had to lie low for a couple of years. But we did make a week-long visit to Istanbul. I distinctly recall chaperoning his mama round while Frederic had a tour of the *hamams*.

We went a few times by ferry across the Strait of Bosporus and enjoyed the beautiful mosques from the Asian side. The oldest mosque, we were told, was the Blue Mosque, which was used for prayers for the first time in 1617. We also ventured to the French novelist Pierre Loti's home, which was on top of a steep hill overlooking the whole of Istanbul. What a fantastic sight. It was thanks to our guide that we got there, since the hill was so steep that he had to jump out of the moving car and put wooden stoppers under its back wheels, and we had to continue to the top on foot.

Topkapi was a palatial residence consisting of four buildings round a courtyard. I was astounded by the lavish opulence and the priceless, handmade carpets. Thereafter came the kitchen building, which impressed me as the head of a house using the modern version. It was antiquated, but still efficient enough to looking after the well-being of the sultan and his guests. Unfortunately I could not see the harem ... it can still be seen, by appointment only. Anyone who would like to have an idea what Istanbul is really like must read Orhan Pamuk's *Istanbul*, a love story between the city and the author.

This was also a time when there were excellent plays appearing in London. Nearly once a week, Frederic's mama came often to have early dinner with me and we went to the theatre. Frederic did not like the spoken word as much as we did; he lived entirely for the world of classical music. We saw stars from the film and theatre worlds, including notable actresses like Ingrid Bergman and Deborah Kerr, and actors from Richard Burton to Ian McKellan. I remember a particularly good performance of *Abelard and Heloise* with Keith Michell and Diana Rigg. After breakfast, Frederic usually collected Mama, and she enjoyed these outings very much.

The well-defined tourist season began to disappear. In earlier years, you could safely say that from September to Easter, London was ours, but that began to change. There were tourists around as much in the months of winter as at any other time of the year. I believe this facilitated the birth of West End musicals, which could be enjoyed by any tourist regardless of his or her command of the English language.

I had a few friends in the club among the members – there was no suggestion of payment in kind – and this type of entertainment was enjoyed by them much more than by myself. I was the everlasting, good-looking escort. We saw everything from *Godspell* (starring David Essex) through *Jesus Christ Superstar* to *Evita* (with Elaine Paige).

One core member of this musical-loving group was a former officer of the Burmese army, retired, and another had been a military instructor to the Sultan of Oman. There was no question of impropriety. Even much later in life, when I was working for a livery hall in the City, the clerk of the company summoned me to his office and demanded an explanation, about my relationship with a colonel in the army of the Omani sultan. The colonel wrote to me on Omani military stationery once or twice a year, to give me the dates of his breaks in London. I asked him in return, "What right do you have to open my mail?"

In the meantime our life at home became more and more pleasant. I redesigned the garden with Frederic's help. It became an oasis in the middle of one of the greatest cities in the world. The garden could no longer be overlooked a few years further on, and we often had our meals outside – and ran for cover when it rained, which it frequently did.

It was during the hot summer of 1975, a very sultry day, when we decided to have a few drinks at lunchtime in our local pub, just up the road. Restrictive opening hours were still in force, and everybody tried to drink as much as possible as quickly as possible on Sundays, since the pubs were open only from noon to 2.00 p.m. and again for a short while later in the evening.

We staggered home, and it was just as well. We had everything prepared for a lunchtime barbecue. We drank more wine and got silly and inebriated. I went to have a shower and, still in my dressing gown, retired to the lounge, lying on the carpet and perusing the Sunday papers.

At some point, I must have fallen asleep, since I did not hear Frederic come into the room. But all of a sudden I woke up feeling a searing pain in my bum. Frederic had entered me, against an agreement we had made many years before. Whatever it was which made him do it was have been driven partly by the alcohol and partly by a long-time wish of his to go all the way and make us a proper couple.

There was nothing I could do or say. The tears ran down my cheeks and an unspeakable sadness came over me. Why, why, why now?

I got up and dressed, and ordered a taxi to take me to my abode in town. I had also had too much to drink, so much that I could not think straight. I just felt numb and very sad. Frederic was the one who always had an enormous appetite for sex. It was important to me, but I did not seem to need it as much as Frederic.

When I woke for the second time on that fateful day, I felt I had stepped out of my body and what had happened had nothing to do with me Well, I was very wrong. I sat up the whole night and pondered. The question of why would not go away.

The following day my private phone must have rung a hundred times, but I was unable to pick it up. I felt like I was sleepwalking. By early afternoon, I had asked the secretary of the club for an audience. I would not disclose the reason, but I told him I needed some time to myself, to come to terms with a very personal problem. By the late afternoon, I was on my way to the airport.

As it happened, the next plane I could catch was to New York, on my favourite airline, TWA. I had just about half an hour to board the plane. Mercifully I slept for most of the flight, having had a sleepless night the day before. I do not remember too many details. It hurt for such a long time. It had happened; where would we go from here?

In the meantime, Frederic had a meeting with the club secretary, who told him that he also was in the dark and did not know where I had gone. But he assured Frederic that I was a responsible young man, and I would come back after a week, as arranged.

I often went to Central Park, or the empty avenues of Manhattan in the middle of the night, dreaming of the days when everything was as it had always been. Maybe it was the right decision, because the turmoil in myself became manageable and I could put the recent hurt on the back burner. "Là ci darem la mano." (I was on the way in offering my hand, my life again).

When I returned to London, I no longer had a reason why I should not pick up my private phone at the club. I think Mama knew that there was a problem. She called to ask whether I would go with her to the theatre to see George Bernard Shaw's play, *Captain Brassbound's Conversion*, with Ingrid Bergman in the cast. Why ever should I not? Mama had no part in our problem; it was only myself who felt betrayed.

When we met, she looked at me with compassion in her eyes and said, "I am so sorry that something unpleasant happened to the two of you, my favourite sons." I still felt an underlying sense of bewilderment. I asked her to tell Frederic that I would contact him when I was ready and composed.

That in part was how I found myself with Frederic at a table in a coffee house at the Serpentine in Hyde Park.

He looked at me and I at him. I was still upset, and Frederic was even worse. He wanted to explain, but I cut him short. "Let us not go over old ground," I said. "We must look forward to a new beginning. Trust is something we will work hard at. It comes with time. We should not take it for granted but keep on working towards it."

As a gesture of conciliation, I handed him an envelope. In it was a booking for the first private tour with Thomas Cook to Egypt. While I was watching the news one evening, Sir Alec Douglas-Home, the British foreign minister, was on an official visit to Egypt. He announced it would soon be possible to visit the country. He was leaning against one of the paws of the Sphinx with the Pyramids as backdrop.

Relations between Britain and Egypt had not been the best since the Suez Crisis in 1956, and this announcement was a boost for the traveller. Christmas 1975 was the date, and all three of us looked forward to the journey tremendously.

The group was kept to fifteen. I remember two Scottish ladies, retired teachers, and a family of three others, parents and son, who could not get their heads out of their guidebooks. They were in sheer bewilderment about the treasures we were going to see.

Flight regulations were not handled to European standards. All our nice English guide, Ann said was, "when the flight is called, run and see that you get a place to sit down." We looked at her in bewilderment. It was true: overbookings were allowed on board, having to stand during the flight and sit down in the gangway for take-off and landing. We could hardly believe it, but it happened, and we carried ten passengers more than we should have done.

We spent a morning discovering Luxor Temple and Karnak. We lunched at the Winter Palace and went by ferry to the eastern bank of the Nile. To our surprise, we were greeted by a very old and distinguished gentleman in a fez and long skirt. His name was Peter, and he had been Howard Carter's personal servant when the grave of King Tut was discovered. He even came back with Carter and served him in London. But one day he couldn't take our British weather anymore and retired. What luck, since he was a mine of information.

In Giza, we went to a *son et lumière* (sound and light show) opposite the Pyramids. It was strange to hear in the English version, the voices of the actors Judi Dench and Richard Burton telling snippets of Egyptian history under the pharaohs.

Mama was a spoilsport when we challenged her to get on a camel. The ride would have been a circle of the Pyramids. At the last moment, the camel turned round and spat at her, and that was the end of her camel ride.

This was on par with our guide in Cairo. After each explanation, he always said, "Look, this is how they did it, and look how they have done it."

Mama and I stayed at the back when we visited Sakkara, the Step Pyramid, and started kicking sand at each other, which got us a severe reprimand from Frederic. On that occasion, Mama felt something more was up and wished to retire after dinner.

Frederic and I went to the all-night bar at the Mena House to discuss our future life together, and once and for all clear the air. Maybe we had Mama in our relationship, and therefore vulnerable to any decision of hers backing one or the other. The evening was almost as it had been when first we met, Frederic and Mandryka. Back then, the evening at the old inn in Bavaria had been perfect with the smell of honeysuckle and jasmine. Here in Egypt, it was the smell of the datura and the brilliant red of the poinsettias. The orange and lemon trees reminded us how far south we had come.

I said to him, "Let's not waste our time in quarrelling and misunderstandings. However, there is one more thing I have to do, Frederic. I will go AWOL for a week at Easter. Don't ask me where I am going and with whom, because I will not tell you. Maybe later?"

I had promised to join my Omani colonel in Aqaba, Jordan, for a week. That was a long time before any international hotel or new buildings had gone up, and the small market town was a haven for scuba divers and people like us with time on our hands. I was not in love with the colonel, but I liked him a lot.

One day we set off for Petra, the rose-red city, which was even more beautiful and serene than I expected. We arrived just as the sun rose, its golden rays falling on the Corinthian pillars of a pink building ahead of us and submerging it in glorious, glowing dawn light.

Continuing through the ruins of the Roman settlement, we saw the gravestones of the former nobility. Somewhat up the hill to our right, there was a rock on which stood the treasury with the same decorative pillars. How could a jewel like this have been forgotten for almost two thousand years? And there my colonel stood in the middle of the well-preserved amphitheatre and recited a poem in Arabic.

I had promised him the trip and did not find the time with him boring or an everyday happening. We parted as good friends and met quite a few times after that. But there was something special, he said, he had never known existed – love.

CHAPTER 9

More of Europe and London

There was still much to see in Europe. The weather had changed for the worse in Yugoslavia, so during the summers we began to explore more and more of Europe. Our first trip took us from London to France. We stayed a few days in Sept Saulx in the Champagne country, followed by a leisurely drive and another overnight stay in Lamotte-Beuvron. We were aiming for the Provence and the famous Roman theatre of Orange.

We had lunch in the foothills of Mount Ventoux, continuing to Avignon, which had a festival going on. There were lots of amusements in and around the town's park, which we could watch from our dusty hotel directly on the green, called aptly L'Horloge, where not only the time had stood still but also the clock had stopped chiming a long time ago.

It was another beautiful, hot summer. We drove via Aix en Provence to Nice, and on to Menton on the border with Italy. We spent the night in Ventimiglia, the birthplace of my predecessor at the club. He had never actually lived there, but during the years he had run the Bengal Club in Calcutta, he invested in two apartments, one for himself and his wife and the other to shore up his pension. The town was not very pretty, compared to Menton, but the hotel was comfortable enough to spend the night. From there we proceeded through northern Italy to the cottage in Croatia. We decided this was enough travelling for one holiday. God willing, we earmarked Tuscany for the next year.

Getting over the border from Italy to Croatia we had the feeling that we were being followed. A motorbike stopped when we did and shadowed us all the way to Zagreb.

A few miles before we reached the town, the bike driver took his camouflage jacket off and put on a jacket with Police written on it in large letters. He flagged us down before we reached the outskirts of Zagreb. Frederic opened his window and asked him what we had done wrong. "Passports at the double," was all the policeman said. His language was rather crude, as in all of the communist satellite states. He gave Frederic's and Mama's passports back, but kept mine. "Police station!" he barked. "Follow me; we want to have a word with your friend."

"Can I come in and translate?" asked Frederic.

"No." Frederic's services were not required, "We have an English translator on our staff."

It was the same old thing – all about my stepfather, whom I rarely even met. When I went to visit the Madonna, she met me in town, and I stayed with her carers.

After a while, when I had tested the waters at my job and knew where I stood and who would support me, I started having dinner with Frederic now and then at the club. He liked a bit of pomp and circumstance while having grouse or pheasant and a glass of vintage Gruaud-Larose. After a while it became a regular visit every week. Apart from some mischievous remarks from the odd member, nobody ever made any direct complaint.

The person who used far more of the club's facilities was my boss, the secretary. He often brought in anything from eight to ten people, mainly freeloaders, shortly after the kitchen closed. When they finished, it would be well on midnight, and the staff left them there with bottles of port and brandy.

Frederic always looked the part when he visited the club, with his blazer and college tie. He was not to be compared to the secretary's guests, who were hairdressers and salesmen in the men's department of Harrods.

One day, the chairman at the time called me into the secretary's office. He gave me the committee meeting's book to read. It was highly unusual that a manager was allowed to see it. At a meeting held under the vice-chairman, my mentor Sir Arthur, some members had referred to the secretary and me as "fairies" and "queens", and said we should be removed.

When I gave the book back to him, he tore out the offending pages and referred to them as unworthy of the club. Quite soon afterwards, Sir Arthur made a show of dining with me once a week in the middle of the dining room, so everybody could see. The rumours, if there were any, stopped for me.

Sir Arthur also encouraged me to do things out of the ordinary. "Where are you going for your holiday?" he asked me once.

I thought for a moment or two and replied mischievously, "I am going off to Kuala Lumpur to watch cricket on the village green."

Goodness knows how often he dined out on this story. It just showed that he had an incredibly good sense of humour. "Och," he would say, "we have this manager at the club, born in Pannonia, who has become more English than the English. He goes off on his holidays to watch cricket on the village green in Kuala Lumpur."

I missed him very much. When he died much too soon, in his early seventies, it was as if my own father had died. In the meantime, however, it became fashionable to dine with the manager and air one's grievances.

My friend Michael, a retired brigadier of the Burmese army – to be precise, the Fourth Gurkha Rifles Brigade – was one of the soldiers posted to Burma and known to be in charge of fierce fighters. They swore an oath of allegiance to the British monarch at the time of their induction. Michael used to give them a yearly dinner at the club, and I always stood them a port or brandy. I looked after them for about ten years. On a very special occasion, I was invited to a private lunch at St. James's Palace with selected soldiers and Michael, given by Queen Elizabeth, the Queen Mother, which was a great honour. She was probably the best raconteur I ever met.

When the lunch was over, Her Majesty stayed on for a short time. Then there was the well-known sound of the gavel, and the toastmaster asked for Her Majesty to be excused, though the gentlemen might stay on for a while if they so wished. Her Majesty wished everybody well. Since the lunch was such a success, my friend Michael got hopelessly drunk. As he was such a big man, it took two of the Gurkhas to get him home to the club, where he usually stayed every week from Tuesday to Friday morning.

I noticed from time to time that Michael had a very dishy young gentleman as dinner guest, who looked like a rugby player. It looked to me that Ruggerboy was with Michael on the same terms as myself, with the exception there was no show, just a sumptuous dinner with good food and expensive wine, even by club standards. They went to the bar after dinner, as was the custom at universities. The participants avail themselves of a jar of beer, sometimes more. Michael was usually legless after such an evening and retired at closing time.

I could never find out until Michael died why he drank so much. When he was discharged from the army, he lived with an ancient and, as I gathered, very possessive mother, whom he was only too glad to leave in Kent during the week while he spent time in London. He could have commuted, but perish the thought. He more than likely did not love her that much, and wanted some sort of private life of his own. On one occasion he blubbered out that he was impotent, but that Ruggerboy and I were the best thing that had happened to him since his discharge from the army. He often felt lonesome.

One evening the inevitable happened. Michael was going to a show with me, and on to a late dinner in a restaurant like Prunier's or the Ivy. As we left the club, who should be coming towards us but Ruggerboy. It was embarrassing for him and me, but Michael was a good talker – when he was sober – and suggested a compromise.

"Why don't we all go to the show and see whether the theatre has any returns, leaving at the interval? The three of us could have dinner in a restaurant of our choice." The play which we only enjoyed up to the interval was *Pygmalion* by George Bernard Shaw, with Diana Rigg as Eliza Doolittle.

After dinner, the question was where would we go from here? Being me, I offered a nightcap in my penthouse, which was not refused. An hour after we arrived at the club, we had to take Michael to his room, heave him onto his bed, and quickly leave. I asked Ruggerboy if he wanted to go home or come back to my pad to finish our nightcap. He answered that he would like the latter, since he was feeling lonely. His wife was expecting their second child in a London hospital, and he was staying with relatives and in no hurry to go home. It was a delightful hour we had on my bed, kissing and cuddling. Just with touching, we came at the same time.

These casual encounters were tolerated by Frederic and me. Our love seemed to be much stronger if they happened shortly before we saw each other again. Often we wanted a complete weekend at home, shut away with our dreams and planning future trips. Then we took the phone off the hook and just vanished from the world.

We made picnic trips to the Chilterns and the Cotswolds, and whole weekend excursions to Anglesey, Tintagel (the site where Tristan and Isolde died), and Devon, which both of us liked very much. We visited the neighbouring counties, where the rolling hills sloped down to the rocky beach. And wherever we went, the whole area reminded me of Thomas Hardy and his description of the landscape, hamlets, and small market towns. Frederic's brother Gerald had written his doctorate on Thomas Hardy, and he often gave me samples of his writings, knowing that I was very interested in the subject and knew almost as much as he did.

In the early seventies, Covent Garden had a renaissance, performing the operas Frederic and I loved to hear. Georg Solti brought *Die Frau ohne Schatten* by Richard Strauss to the Garden, as well as his *Salome*, *Arabella* (with Mandryka), and *Der Rosenkavalier*. We saw Puccini's finest work, *Turandot*, with Joan Sutherland as Turandot. The list of performances we enjoyed is far too long to mention all.

On a very hot evening during an Indian summer in London, Frederic invited me to *The Flying Dutchman*, which he loved most of Wagner's operas. We saved money and did not buy a programme, since we preferred purchasing a drink during the interval. Entering the theatre, we saw an effeminate crowd making quite a racket with their shrieks of laughter. I asked Frederic how come the limp wristed had turned out to see a Wagner opera? He also could not fathom it.

We were seated and expected to hear the *Dutchman's* overture. Instead, we got the lilting strains of *Swan Lake*. Frederic had got the week wrong. Luckily we had seats at the gangway, and we left presently. Frederic had his strong likes and dislikes, and among the latter was the ballet. We also dined out on this story many times.

CHAPTER 10

The Munich Summer

One day in early spring, between opening the curtains and hurrying for the loo, I thought, "Aren't we lucky to have such a homey maisonette?" The sun shone, and Frederic's room was flooded with light. It was unusual for him not to get up after he had opened the curtains and left the door ajar. I looked in his room, and he pretended to be asleep. I thought, "Well, I will get you up in no time." I crawled under his duvet and started tickling him. He burst into laughter and threatened to throw me out of his bed if I carried on bothering him. We both looked at the bright room and were happy that we had an uninterrupted view through the French doors of our garden.

It was my morning, and I made my way to the kitchen to make breakfast. Here as well, the sun shone as brightly as possible. The birds in the garden serenaded us with their pleasant twitter. That is how our days began when we were at home together and the sun was shining.

This was also a day off work for me, since I wanted to go to see the Hotel and Catering Show at the Olympia. Frederic had to teach at the Royal Academy of Music, having taken the extra honour on when his professor was asked if he knew a native-speaking German who also had some musical background. After coaching his students, he did not have to go back to the university for the rest of the day. He was enjoying teaching correct German pronunciation to the young singers. One of his pupils was Aled Jones.

In 1980, Frederic was made an Honorary Associate Member of the Royal Academy of Music, of which the Queen Mother was a patron. She bestowed the honour on Frederic. I was glad that he had been recognised as such a good teacher, and that his Mama and I could be there when the certificate was handed to him by Princess Alexandra, who also at one time studied the piano at the academy. Just before Frederic retired from the academy in the early twenty-first century, he met Katherine Jenkins, who came to study at the academy at 17 years old. On the odd occasion, he tutored her as well. He had that rare gift of being charming and a fine teacher too.

Somewhere along the line, Frederic had made it in a foreign land – just as I had, but in quite a different way. Maybe this was also a reason why we got on so well. Frederic remained a German subject while enjoying the trimmings of the monarchy. I swore the oath of allegiance, since I was after jobs which I would not have got otherwise. We were a much-requested pair among our friends, and often invited to lunch or dinner in restaurants and the homes of friends.

We also entertained quite often at home. I was responsible, usually, for the minor tasks. Frederic was a much better cook then I, his inheritance from his Viennese mama. I was responsible for the table and the drinks. At a time when most people were offering a variety of drinks, we only ever served medium-dry sherry or, on special occasions, champagne.

This was based on a tip from my mentor at the club: do not let invited guests have three or more glasses of whisky or gin, which will kill off their taste buds. Then you might as well serve them McDonald's takeaway. After the meal it was brandy, port, or Tokay. These were my mentor's points of advice for giving a successful lunch or dinner party. Every summer, I was invited to a lunch at his manor house near Juniper Hill in Surrey, together with his family. These events were always much enjoyed by my host and myself. Unfortunately for all concerned, there was never any evidence that my boss, the club secretary, was ever invited.

As it often happens in England, when the sun shines brightly first thing in the morning, there is no guarantee she won't disappear half an hour later. By the time I made my way to the exhibition, it was pelting down, and many an umbrella had been lost to the gusts of strong wind which accompanied the rain. There was my morning walk from Earls Court to Olympia gone; I had to take the tube. What a nuisance! I was looking forward to a day at the exhibition, and in the evening Frederic and I were going to a concert at the Royal Festival Hall.

At Olympia I met quite a few people from the trade whom I knew from various seminars and health and safety meetings. Perusing the new kitchen gadgets and various other exhibits, I wandered over to the show kitchen, where chefs cooked. One could watch them trying out new recipes; one could also sample the dishes. I always looked forward to this part of the show.

Among the chefs were a lot of young and ambitious cooks. I found one of them particularly interesting. He was a picture-postcard version of a good-looking young man, in a very English sort of way – a mixture of Michael York and Simon MacCorkindale. I thought that whoever got him, male or female, would be in luck if his temperament complemented his looks.

About a week later, having not an awful lot to do, I thought I would look in on the show again and see if he was still there. He was, and I asked him if he had time to have a jar or two after his performance.

Frederic was then away in Munich, where his Mama had been hospitalized. He would come to London to stay with me for a weekend here and there, but Mama had a serious problem and was still not well enough to return. I flew to Munich whenever possible, since not only did his mama need him there, but I also missed him in London very much. We stayed in a flat in Munich that belonged to the lady who had given me refuge in the mountain village during our fathers' witch hunt years before.

Mama did not leave the hospital until October. Frederic's professor gave him a sabbatical because he knew how much Mama meant to Frederic. I, in the meantime, was very bored without him, and did some things I am not too proud of.

At the appointed time, my young chef turned up, and we had a few beers together. All I told him was how much I liked his work and how pleasant it was just to watch him cook. His face flushed with embarrassment. It turned out that he worked for another club, albeit one which was not known to me.

We chatted very pleasantly, and I nearly forgot that I was supposed to pick up Frederic from the airport and I better had to get a move on.

Looking at my watch, I could not believe how quickly the time had passed. I had to set off immediately. "Sorry I kept you," said my young man. "Would you like to meet again?"

I said, "Yes. Please give me your telephone number and I will ring you."

Even though we were nearing our twentieth anniversary, Frederic and I still missed each other's company when we were apart. Often when we turned our memory clocks back, it was still, "When first we met, he called me Mandryka".

In the intervals of what seemed like my jetting off every five minutes to Munich, I enjoyed the company of other members of the club who definitely were heterosexual. One in particular was named Philip, but behind his back the members called him Mr Dunbar, the name of a well-known British investment house in the seventies and eighties. Doing business in the club with other members was against the house rules, but he tried to sell savings schemes and life insurance to everybody in sight. As it turned out in my case, I made quite a bit of money from the Canadian stock exchange.

He had an eye for the ladies all right, and on one occasion we got thrown out of Tramp's in Jermyn Street when a scuffle broke out between him and another punter. On another occasion, being there in the early hours of the morning, we encountered Princess Margaret in somewhat louche company. But she looked every inch a princess. And since we were not exactly sober, we were in no position to criticize.

Strangely, though Philip was all over the beauties of the night, he never took any of them to a hotel. Nor did he pursue the women at the Gaslight Club in St. James's, where the ladies in the prostitution game were much lower class than the ones at Tramp's. These girls used clubs as cover to work from, and had no trouble with the police. I now think it could have been that he enjoyed the nep, buying the girls coloured lemonade while he got drunk on the champagne. Much later, another member told me Philip was impotent and got his kicks that way.

After almost three weeks, I thought to ring my young chef. He was slightly miffed, since I had waited for such a long time without a word, and the phone messages from him that were handed to me did not prompt me to ring him any sooner. He wanted to cook a meal, just for the two of us, in his flat in Elephant and Castle. I had heard of the place, but one did not go there; I did not know anyone who lived there. He said he would pick me up at seven o'clock. It was just a short walk to his home.

We relaxed and talked while he made preparations for the meal. We had a couple of glasses of claret, since he, like me, drank beer only now and then and never any spirits.

The meal was superb. It made up for the shabby state the flat was in, with falling stucco and plasterwork. He was as pleasant as he looked, and we had plenty to talk about. We lounged around on the couch together – not the casting one, but one I chose.

Before going to bed, I rang the night porter at the club and told him I would be staying out. I gave him the chef's number to ring in case of any trouble or accident. Unfortunately or fortunately for the club, there was a clause in my contract which stated that if I wished to be out for the night, this was only possible with the secretary's permission. He then would be contacted in case of any problem. Although I was in breach of my contract, I knew that I would not be snitched on by the staff who were as loyal to me as I always was towards them.

There came the day when Frederic was returning home and I had to drop my young chef. I feared the day when I had to tell him. But I did, and he went unusually quiet. Then he asked, "Why did you not tell me before that you had a steady boyfriend?"

What could I say? That I had let him wait at the beginning, and wait he had, even when I did not take any notice of the messages he left at the club? I couldn't excuse my bad behaviour, knowing I was wrong. There was and always would be Frederic.

Frederic came back with Mama in tow, smiling like a Cheshire cat, and I was pleased to see her restored to her former health.

CHAPTER 11

The East

Slowly we overcame our cash flow problems. Having itchy feet, I started to do travel research behind Frederic's and Mama's backs. In those days, you went on tours arranged by travel agents, not by a click on the PC. I settled on a whistle-stop tour with Kuoni, bringing East and West together in a couple of weeks. The tour was slightly costly, but I thought the three of us could just manage it.

Before we started the journey, I had to sell the arrangements to Mama and Frederic. Mama was on my side; I was sure of that. Frederic had to be convinced that the time spend in faraway places would not be wasted, since the trip had been put together with art and culture in mind, not just landmarks and tourist attractions. Our route was this: departure London; first stopover, New Delhi; on to Kathmandu, Bangkok, and Teheran; return to London.

Frederic's feelings were lukewarm. He did not think that beyond the continent of Europe there was any noticeable culture which he would appreciate, even though he had simply loved Egypt. Geography and the history of foreign cultures were more my forte. I won, and the trip got booked. We were really excited – even Frederic, after he studied the guidebooks and found that there was culture after all, the rich cultural heritage of the Far East and on the subcontinent of India.

It proved true that when you start travelling long haul, problems occur which are nobody's fault. Our plane was in position for departure when all flights out of Heathrow were delayed due to heavy fog. When the fog lifted, the crew had to be changed. By the time the new crew arrived, the fog had come back as well. All told, we waited in the plane for almost six hours. It was Christmas time and the authorities would not admit passengers from waiting planes back into the lounges, since they were already overcrowded.

Thank God we had bought some wine at the duty free, which we drank with the meal that was served during our waiting time. We always travelled with a corkscrew, since searches were not as strict then as they are today.

The only glimmer of hope we had came when the new captain came on board. He said that we would try to get airborne in the wake of the Concorde departing for New York. The supersonic airliner pushed the fog aside long enough that another plane had sufficient light for take-off. It worked; we departed eight hours late, and six hours since boarding the plane to New Delhi.

On our first outing to a temple, we really did not have a clue how the Hindu religion worked. There was a great deal of razzmatazz about it: snake charmers at the entrance, heavy incense hanging in every corner of the temple. There were also so many gods to pray to, from Shiva to Parvathi, and last but not least Ganesh, the elephant god. The ladies floated about in their colourful saris. There were garlands of marigolds everywhere. Various other offerings, like food and drink displayed in silver or gold chalices in front of the deities, reminded me of a book I read quite a few years later, *City of Djinns* by William Dalrymple. He described Delhi so atmospherically that I seriously wished to be as good a writer as he is.

The next morning we ventured to Chandni Chowk in the old city. It was full of people and gold and silver jewellery shops. A young man came towards us dressed in a white Hindu habit; he was unusually tall for an Indian, and so beautiful that many people just stood staring at him. I must say, it nearly knocked me over just to look at him before the crowd swallowed him. The place, with the most old-fashioned restaurants, was a delight for Mogul food lovers and strictly alcohol-free. All three of us loved the *lassi*, a yogurt drink, with our meals.

We admired Edwin Lutyens's architecture, including the All India War Memorial as well as the parliament buildings. The latter had an almost pink appearance which went well with the draught and dust before the heavy monsoon storms. The Fort in Old Delhi looked majestically behind the heavy fortification when the main gate was open and gave an unrivalled view of the fort's beauty itself. Once the doors were closed, you seemed to be in another world. There were water fountains and pavilions all made of marble, and as in most places, the air was full of incense and marigolds.

There was only one thing missing, according to our Indian guide – the Peacock Throne, which the last Shah of Persia acquired. His title was closely connected to the throne, which was built in the seventeenth century and had a very chequered history in Mogul India. Built under the reign of Nadir Shah, it was transported to the fierce land of the Kurds, dismantled, and brought back to the Indian capital. It proved impossible to reassemble the old throne, and a copy was made to resemble the original.

The following day was a very long one, to see Agra and the Red Fort as well as the Taj Mahal, which was a fair distance away. Frederic found a very interesting piece of information in one of the guidebooks, referring to the ghost town of Fatehpur Sikri. The town was completely intact, but the water wells had dried up and the whole population had left. It was awesome.

From the ramparts of an old temple, a young boy jumped from the top – about thirty feet high – into what seemed to have been an old wooden washing vessel, which did not appear at all big or high enough. For a few rupees, he would oblige his audience and do it all over again.

Shortly after that we saw a wedding procession taking place, with elephants and a throne for the married couple. It was one of the most colourful events imaginable.

We ended up forking out quite a lot of money to get down to Fatehpur Sikri and make the excursion of about half an hour. Neither of our regular guides would go. They said that the road was full of potholes and the driver would not drive us there. Then the guides, one Indian and one English, got into an argument, right in front of the unforgettable Taj Mahal. We were either to visit a marble factory, with the obligatory gift shop, or a very colourful market near the Red Fort.

Now we got angry, and a honeymooning young couple, with whom we had become very friendly, joined us. If you have money, you have no problems in India. A bystander took us to Fatehpur Sikri for a hefty price. None of us knew whether we would be back again in time to meet up with our tour, but we paid the asking price. It was worthwhile, having come that far. We had no desire to see a marble factory or a market from which the guides got a percentage of the proceeds, and where the merchants tried to persuade you that most of their stock were antiques, omitting to mention it had all been made a week ago in a back alley.

On the return to Agra, we barely caught our bus. Both of the guides were annoyed that we got to go where we wanted to go in the first place. Driving in India is a harrowing business, but driving at night looks just suicidal. There was only one lane of road. When there was oncoming traffic, whoever had the better nerves drove on, and the other landed in a ditch. Finally, after an extremely bumpy ride, we arrived back in Delhi.

The following morning we were to check out, and Mama came to our room slightly distressed. About seven servants were standing outside her door and begging very noisily for baksheesh. I went up to see them and asked what they had done. "Master I filled the bathtub when memsahib wanted a bath." The jobs they did or were supposed to have done did not surprise me, and they went away having got their share.

After fighting our way through the crowds and the never-ending number of cows blocking the way, we arrived at the airport. Thank God we made it and the plane to Kathmandu was waiting for us. Our first sight upon leaving the Hindu population behind was a smile and a *wai* (the Buddhist greeting) from our stewardesses.

Once the doors were closed and we were airborne, the demand for drinks started. In an hour and a half, the supposedly abstinent Indian passengers had drunk the bar dry. Soon we were flying towards the Himalayas and could see Mount Everest, snow-capped, its glaciers flickering in the bright sunlight. I was in heaven, passing Mount Everest with my lover Frederic and our Mama by my side.

When we touched down, we could see miles of paddy fields, and the air was pure and fragrant. After barely two hours' flight, the world had another face to show us. Nepal is a small kingdom high up in the Himalayas. Its capital is Kathmandu, where the "flower children" still existed, wearing flowers in their hair and long, billowing native dresses. There were also some gurus at the temple of the palace, but their time was running out.

We stayed in a hotel where most windows faced the yard, quiet enough to let us have some rest when we felt like it. It was magic when we stayed in Mama's room, which was one of the very few with a window. It overlooked the palace garden and the large temple complex. Day and night, wind chimes could be heard, and the smell of incense once again hung over the town.

Atop the hotel was a roof garden with a view of the mountains, and we spent a few days having our sundowners on the roof. We even got up at three o'clock one morning, to be driven along a quite hazardous road to a vantage point, where we saw the sun rising behind Nagarkot and the majestic Mount Everest.

Our Sri Lankan neighbours in London had a young lady in their family who was married to a royal minor in Kathmandu. Ringing her, we were invited to high tea at the palace one day.

Next to the palace was the house of the living goddess, who could be seen sometimes at the window, to the delight of the many sightseers who specially came to see her. The living goddess was usually a girl of great beauty, chosen at about 10 years old. She was worshipped as the descendant of the Hindu goddess of power, Durga. Once she entered puberty, however, her status reverted to that of a normal human, and another young girl was chosen to be the living goddess. At the time it was rumoured that living goddesses were likely to end up as prostitutes because the young men would shy away from a girl who was spoiled rotten; however more recently, research has shown that most of the girls do marry and in any event receive government pensions.

Much to our disappointment, when we revisited Kathmandu years later, it had become an Indian slum. I have banished that visit from my memory; I think of it only as it was when we were there first.

Since we had such good weather in Nepal, we made a lot of excursions. One was to Boudhanath, where the Gurkha soldiers were trained. On to the stupa with the large Buddhist eyes, Swayambhunath were a lot of Tibetan monks were working on *tangkas*. These are temple flags that most people also have in their homes. The flags have pictures of the Ramayana or other Buddhist deities, mostly bodhisattvas painted on canvas with multicoloured linen surrounds.

I often looked at Frederic, and his face was full of approval when we saw a memorable sight. In Nepal they seemed to be everywhere. The mystique of the Far East was so strong, together with the high altitude, that we got light-headed in awe of the beauty of the place.

There was a monkey temple, Mygoda, next to the river Bagmati, and the monkeys there seemed to have Mama on their minds. Every place we went, in no time she had one sitting on her shoulder. I'm sorry that I cannot adequately describe her face. She did not think it was funny, while Frederic and I could not stop laughing.

On the embankment of the river, there was a funeral pyre still burning for the mother of the ruling monarch, who had died a week before we arrived in Kathmandu.

One last story of another monkey temple. This one was quite high up, 200 steps or more and over 2,000 years old. The steps had railings on the outside. Luckily they never needed polishing: the monkeys glide down them like children down banisters, and kept them clean. We heard about this from many people, and we were very much in luck to see this spectacle even though we were there just a short time. And this time Mama was spared from gaining a friend, since we kept to the background. The monkeys decided on ladies nearby, who also thought it was funny!

Our next stop was Bangkok, which was the first city we encountered in the Far East that seemed to cater to the visitor. More than elsewhere, it had a little modern veneer. The town itself was not the most beautiful we saw. But it was unrivalled in its temple district, with Thammasit University at the entrance. There were all the famous temples: the temple of the Emerald Buddha, the famous temple Wat Pho, the temple of the reclining Buddha, and, across the river, glittering in the sunshine, Wat Arun, the temple of the dawn.

As it happened then and has continued to happen to the present day, the Thai military was in charge. All towns and cities had a curfew imposed on them, beginning at midnight and ending at six o'clock in the morning. Groups over five were not allowed to gather. The military was everywhere. So Frederic and I thought, "This is the end of our pub crawl. No good trying to have a look at the talent."

But as always, Mama could feel that we wanted to go out. She agreed, for the few days we were there, to have an early dinner, which allowed us time to go out afterwards and return before the curfew. All the bars then in the Far East had short-time rooms attached, which were very much in demand. And don't you believe they were there only for the tourists; they were also busy with Far Eastern men.

This let us stomach our time in the tourist traps during the day – a python fighting with a mongoose, or a trip to the floating market. To make the day, there was always the Rose Garden and since Thais can't pronounce the letter *R*, their praise sounded to us like "lose galden vely nice".

Our last destination was Teheran, the best part of the journey location-wise. We stayed at the Hilton with a wonderful sight of the Elbrus Mountains. There in the foothills the Shah had his residence, since it was impossible to protect him from insurgents in the palace in town.

We had a visit to the souk, which was totally devoid of visitors other than our little group. On another day there was quite a lot of activity towards the palace; the occasion was a state visit by the President of Pakistan. The Golestan Palace was in a pitiful state and desperately needed refurbishment. So did the town's waste-water treatment. Sewage flowed on the surface next to the pavement.

Where had all the oil money gone? One possible explanation was in all Western newspapers: the Shah ordered all casinos in the south of France, openly, to stop his sister Ashraf from gambling when her losses reached half a million pounds in one night.

Our last visit was to the winter mosque in Teheran, which was a marble-covered, vast domed mosque underground, full of priceless handmade carpets, one more beautiful than the other.

Again we were often in the company of the young honeymoon couple, who discovered an Armenian restaurant that was fairly cheap and also served wine. Most places were dry, but our hotel had a regular crowd of wealthy Iranians, who used the bar and the restaurant frequently.

We would have loved to see more, but unfortunately the time was too short. We went to the airport at the same time as the President of Pakistan was leaving. The airport was closed for an hour for his convenience, and we sweated in the sun, in a bus without air conditioning.

CHAPTER 12

Interlude with a Doctor

This journey set the pattern for our travelling. We had been caught by the real travel bug. Mama often travelled with us until, in the early 1990s, she died. In the two years leading up to that, we had to restrict ourselves to short-haul flights to Tunisia or Morocco. She said goodbye rather early, on the night leading up to her seventieth birthday. The only real consolation was that she had all her children around her. Gerald was in England on a trip from Washington, staying with his sister in Manchester, and Frederic was summoned up the day before.

One fine spring day in the late 1970s, Frederic and I set off to the mountains. I had built up another ten holiday days per year, one for every year I worked for the club. Often there were work commitments which I could not leave unattended, but with inflation rising as high as 28 per cent for a while, money was not readily available for parties, luncheons, or dinners, even among our members.

We felt the lure to spend Easter in a Catholic country, for which Easter is the most revered holy day. We attended a procession to the *kreuzgang*, or Stations of the Cross, marking the pivotal moments of Christ's sufferings. The markers were mounted up a forest lane, with a chapel at the end of it. The priest asked for forgiveness and blessed all of us attending.

It was the time of the Föhn, a warm wind from the Sahara which now and then travels across Spain or France and gets trapped in the Austrian or Bavarian mountain valleys. On Lake Chiemsee, not very far from the border between Germany and Austria, the authorities gave permission for an early start to the boating season, allowing pleasure boats to be taken out of mothballs.

I imagine many people know of the existence of König Ludwig II of Bavaria, the mad king, and his love of castle building. Lake Chiemsee is a beautiful setting for one such castle, which unfortunately was never finished. It would have rivalled any of the others. It is situated on an island in the lake called Herrenchiemsee, where concerts were given by candlelight in a mirror hall resplendent with crystal chandeliers.

We walked a wide, pretty footpath with age-old chestnut trees. At the end, we took a boat and went to a smaller island, which was called Frauenchiemsee. It had a wonderful restaurant, where we ate quite a few times in a homely garden full of old-fashioned flowers sampling the early sun.

Frederic started reminiscing about the days when first we met, and I could only support him. We were approaching twenty-five years together, and we were still holding hands under the table as we had so many years ago. Both of us were still in love with each other – perhaps more deeply so than ever.

We stayed with Frederic's and Mama's friends. They ran a bed and breakfast on the ground floor of their spacious house and always had room for us. The husband was a teacher at the school where Mama had also taught. She had spoken for him when a vacancy turned up. He looked after pupils in their last years before their schooling ended for good; it needed a man of substance to keep the older pupils in order.

Frederic's and his siblings' house had to be sold. Their father had made a mess of his will and given a quarter of the property to his son from his first marriage. Gerald got another quarter in his father's will and a third of his mother's share in her will. Frederic's sister was not interested in keeping the house. Frederic was in no position to buy the others out. We were only just comfortable in London, and there was no money available to spend holding on to a house in the mountains which might be visited once a year by one or another of the siblings. Much to Frederic's regret, first we had to give up the cottage in Yugoslavia during the wars, and then he had to sell the house in the mountains.

These were only the beginning of changes in Frederic's world. It was a world which he could no longer absorb. Of course he had a brilliant mind, but he hated anything changing. The last straw was when we moved from the ground-floor maisonette to the first floor. He wanted to keep the garden, and could not foresee that anybody buying the maisonette on the first floor would turn the huge loft space into a granny flat, or a small self-contained apartment. This happened because the house, being at the end of a terrace, was double fronted, and the attic was unusually large. He agreed that it was common sense, but still could not believe that it would have a huge impact on our life downstairs.

Frederic bought me my first computer and was also willing to pay for a computer course, since we agreed that one or the other of us probably would need it one day professionally. This became the case for Frederic, as he had accepted a position with the International Baccalaureate, which took off in a big way. He was supervisor for German, head of a team of four people, marking papers and listening to conversations and marking these as well.

As the years went by, the team grew to satisfy the demand for ever more teachers. When Frederic retired, he had sixteen teachers to supervise and organize. He had to give up the job when it started getting at him physically as well as mentally. I was the only one who knew what was involved, since I typed lots of reports and mark-ups for what would later become a completely paperless baccalaureate.

Of course the money was always welcome, but the salary he earned was barely more than slave labour. And on the occasions when we worked together, we often had a quarrel, since he did not understand the workings of the computer fully and often blamed me for being too quick for him to follow.

Whenever we went to the Bavarian mountains, we met up with Frederic's lady friend who had sheltered me during the time our fathers were waging war against us. She noticed that I had a bad bout of hay fever, which I had every year, and took me to her "witch doctor", a practitioner of alternative medicine, who believed his concoctions were much better than any manufactured pills. He got me a two month's course of herbal injections, which cured me forever of hay fever. I never suffered from it again.

These injections had to be given into my buttocks, and I was not quite sure if I could do this myself. I tried a few times and failed. A word from the club secretary shed light on my problem. Not far away was a private general practitioner who had recently employed an NHS-qualified assistant. "I know him only from the telephone," the secretary said. "I have not seen him. Why don't you make an appointment with him? Ask if he is willing to treat the live-in staff, and we will pay him a retainer on top of his NHS salary."

I was grateful for the advice. At the same time I could raise the question of whether he would give me the injections in the morning before treatment hours.

I climbed up to the second floor to see him at his surgery. When he opened the door, I was speechless. He was a carbon copy of the American actor James MacArthur, Danno from the famous cop series *Hawaii Five-O*.

I raised the question of the injections with him. His answer was that he would do it for me, and he would not hear of any charges. The first injection gave me such a hard-on that I could scarcely button up my trousers. Oh dear. And I would have this happen every morning for the next two months?

In the beginning we resorted to small talk, and I did not know how far we could go. After all, I did not know much about him, nor did he know about me. One day he asked me if I ever got any free time in the evenings. He had been given two tickets to *The Pirates of Penzance*, a Gilbert and Sullivan operetta. Of course it was a D'Oyly Carte Opera Company production at the Savoy Theatre, which D'Oyly Carte had built with these plays in mind.

I have to admit, I was a bit nervous and yet hoped to make a good impression on him. I did not think of a love affair, and I think neither did he. We had a pleasant evening, even though I could not warm to this kind of entertainment. After the show we went to a pub in Drury Lane, home of the Covent Garden vegetable and flower market as well as the Royal Opera House. We ordered a snack and a glass of wine. By the time we had a second glass, we really threw all our inhibitions to the wind and talked openly of what both of us had been thinking on and off for quite a while now.

Again I had an affair brewing in the background. The question was not if, it was more where and when.

When all the injections had been given, I invited him for dinner at the club and introduced him to the secretary. The following morning, I happened to be in the secretary's office to discuss some business, and he looked at me hard. "Sebastian, you are playing with fire. What do you mean? Don't tell me this is an innocent friendship. Either you have started already, or you will be before long."

"How do you know?"

"Well, I watched you and him at dinner. Your way of communicating with each other said more than if you had told me."

"I am sorry it was so obvious."

"Don't be sorry. I don't think other people were sufficiently observant or interested, and you did nothing wrong. It was just the body language which gave the two of you away."

There was an August holiday on the way. My doctor had some commitments, and I flew to Venice to meet up with Frederic. We spent a few days in Venice, since I had never been there. We by then had been to Florence of course, and Tuscany in general, but Venice was a first time for me. What shall I say? Every place that is beautiful anyway looks twice as good in the sunshine.

Of course I had to make an excursion to the beach, remembering Thomas Mann's *Der Tod in Venedig*. In summer it looked too overcrowded to be a place for an ageing man to chase after a young boy in a melancholy, late summer setting. (Remember Gustav?)

Gradually we made our way to the cottage on the island, which we still had then. We were looking forward to slumming it for a while. It was great fun, since all of us were people who enjoyed fun and sunshine. There was the usual stormy weather from time to time, but on the whole the weather held remarkably well.

Even then, Yugoslavia had an uneasy feeling, and it looked like any day there might be trouble. As on previous occasions, I had my obligatory grilling from the Zagreb police. I dearly wished they would leave me alone. We experienced shadowing on the island, on our way to visit our friend from Bavaria who had also a peasant dwelling on the other side of the village. She was grilling steaks and making fresh salads.

When it was time to eat, the steaks were bloody and not very nice. Sitting on the terrace wall, we fed the steaks to our friend's little dachshund Vipsy. She remarked the following day when we met that she could not understand what had happened to her pet. He had been sick all night and brought up an unusual amount of undigested meat. "I better watch him next time," she said, "and make sure he is not pinching meat from the plate next to the grill."

The days passed all too quickly, as they did every year, and I had to say goodbye to Frederic and Mama. They were going to tour Bohemia, and he would again not be back until the beginning of October.

There also was a further irritant: the island's brand-new airport, built for tourists to Dalmatia. This airport was intended to serve passengers getting off the plane in Zagreb, connecting to the airport on the island and right down to Dubrovnik by the very scenic mountain road, with a shuttle bus meeting every flight. Under the rule of Slobodan Milosevic, this connection was mothballed, much to the annoyance of the Croats. You had to fly to and from Belgrade on a very expensive Yugoair ticket and spend five or six hours each way in a boring airport transit lounge with nothing to do. Then you flew back to Zagreb and finally to London. This was torture. I was not fond of the Serbs anyway, and by God they needed the tourists for foreign currency.

Arriving back at Heathrow and the club, I wished I were a week older, since the first few days were mostly spent sifting through letters and memoranda, trying to prioritise the backlog and just beavering away. My afternoon telephonist, Lilly, who was with me for a long time, watched over me and decided who got through. None of the members had the number of my private line, which I hid in a drawer of my desk.

A few days after my arrival, James the doctor rang – he not only looked like James MacArthur, he also shared his Christian name. Now that there were no more injections to be given, where would we go from here?

Family problems had arisen for him during the summer. His wife had asked for a divorce, and demanded to be the guardian of the two children. There was no objection on his side; he could not begin to think of looking after a toddler and a 5-year-old girl. For a moment I felt a pang of regret, but this subsided. If it hadn't been me, it probably would have been someone else.

I had not told him about Frederic. James often asked why a good-looking man like me was completely unattached: "I don't believe it." I had to own up some time, and now was as good as any other time. Since our meetings were to stop when Frederic got back to England, they were bittersweet meetings. There was never any future for the two of us.

I had not thought of things like that when I met him. I had not even considered a serious affair a possibility during the time when we were saying nothing of our private lives. If he had not been so damned pretty, it would have been easier, but I had never settled for second best.

For six weeks, I comforted him during the divorce proceedings. He had made up his mind he was quitting the NHS to work for a pharmaceutical company, which offered him twice the money the NHS paid.

That, incidentally, was the end of the club's GP. We had to find another one, which we eventually did. It was not very far from the notorious Centre Point Building. He did a whole waiting room of twenty to thirty people in an hour or two. "What is the matter with you?" the doctor would greet everybody. "Tell me, and I give you a prescription and see you in one or two weeks' time. If you have any more problems, you can always go to Accident and Emergency in the next hospital." Pity there was no alternative solution to James.

James and I met a few times that September. He was just like Frederic, hungry for sex all the time; sometimes I just could not keep up with him. At the end of the summer, he handed me an envelope with an airline ticket for a long weekend in Marrakech. We were to stay at the La Mamounia, where Churchill used to stay; some copies of his paintings were displayed in the corridors. The service and the ambience were that of a hundred years ago. The fountains still played in the central courtyard, and hushed voices from the past told stories. The wind of time had settled over the hotel.

That's where we spent most of our time – first with coffee, then a glass of wine. We had been to the souk and also to the square of Djem el Fnaa. That was enough of sightseeing for us. We had not come to see the sights, but to talk about us. James believed there still could be a future for us.

Sometimes I looked at him, and he at me, and we regretted not having met earlier in our lives. But I would never leave Frederic again. Like any other couple, we had our ups and downs, but we remained true to each other. Occasional cheating was tolerated by both of us.

James could not understand our attitude and the way Frederic and I dealt with each other. He wanted so desperately to have a long-standing friendship with me, to grow up in each other. But that was not what I wanted, because I had it already. I might stray, but I never wanted to live with another friend.

I said, "I wish, James, that I could give you a straight answer. I can only blame myself for being promiscuous. I will never be able to give you an answer you might want. Frederic and I go back a very long time, and I will be forever in love with him."

"But why? He obviously spends his university holidays only partly with you and the rest with his Mama."

"And that is part of the sticking point: we never have the time to get bored with each other. And as with you, he and I often differ in opinion. We can get quite hot under the collar when debating a subject. You have an Anglo-Saxon attitude in music, books and art, and you have a narrow knowledge of middle Europe."

But all this was a smokescreen I felt I had to create, since I did not wanted him to carry any excess emotional baggage about me into his new life.

We parted on our arrival at Heathrow and heard nothing from each other for quite a few years. Then one day towards the end of lunch, I received a message from the porter that a gentleman by the name of James was in the smoking room, waiting for me.

Indeed there he was, and I would have hardly recognised him in the street. He had aged so much, as one only did when having huge problems with family, work, or life. I was glad to see him, but since we had parted, he had gone from one problem to another and needed to go to rehab for a drinking problem. What could I say? It was written all over his face: he was deeply unhappy. We met up a few more times, but the flame could never be re-ignited.

Chapter 13

Many Journeys

Not long after Mama's death, my own mother, the Madonna, died, and the airlines lost one of their regular passengers to Munich. My mother ended her days in Kufstein, and the best way for me to get there had been to hire a car in Munich, take the Inntal motorway to Rosenheim in Bavaria, and turn in the direction of Innsbruck. There, just over the border with Germany, was Kufstein.

The Madonna still had some personal jewellery. She stipulated in her will that this should go to her granddaughter in Cariboo Country, Williams Lake, Canada, where my half-sister lived. I booked the trip with Trailfinders, an Australian company, who had just two branches in London. They were known for tailor-made travel, as our trip required. The girl who liaised with us found my request to visit Williams Lake very strange. Her comment was, "Why on earth would you want to go there?"

"Family."

She apologized.

The rest of Mama's jewellery came to me; I took it straight to a pawn shop.

While Frederic enjoyed himself in Vancouver, I had to deal with the family. My half-sister, whom I had not seen for years, was welcoming to me as she could be. At home in our youth, I had longed for her friendship, but she had none to give, since she was the go-between between our mother and father.

My niece appeared to be highly strung due to the isolation; her nearest schoolmate was miles away. The youngsters had sleep-overs, since it was impossible for them to see each other on the weekend unless their parents brought them by car and picked them up a day later.

My brother-in-law was a man who had grown up as an orphan. He had a passion for pistol shooting and a vast collection of classical music. His den was full of trophies he had won in pistol shooting.

Three days of family life brought back bad memories. I was glad to leave and be picked up by Frederic, and ever so glad to catch the next plane back to Vancouver.

Leaving Vancouver, we flew to San Francisco and had a few pleasant days in the city of Armistead Maupin. Whatever he wrote was even at the best of times an understatement. On one or more occasions I told Frederic that this kind of life was a dance on a volcano, that punishment would have to follow – and it did, in the form of AIDS.

After the high life in San Francisco, we boarded a plane to Sydney. What a difference! The place looked and breathed the great times under the British Empire, and yet it was very vibrant. It seemed to fit in with the Anglo-Saxon mind and temperament. Gay pride was a very long way off, and yet the people were friendly and helpful. It was a recipe for having a good time without getting involved in the scene.

From there we went to Tokyo. Japan was a country I had always wanted to visit, and now we were there. We stayed in a traditional, old-fashioned place called Anabashi Riokan. It had gliding paper doors and windows, just as you see in many stage sets for *Madama Butterfly*, the well-known opera by Puccini. The bedroom had bedrolls on the floor and a traditional Japanese bath, made of wood, in which you could sit down and wash yourself. There was neither a key to the entrance nor the bedroom. When we enquired about security, the clerk on the reception told us that, should anyone break in, they would be caught, named, and shamed in their own neighbourhood. Thus we stowed our valuables and passports in our suitcases, which we kept locked, much to the amusement of the clerk.

Then came the big event: we boarded the bullet train, the Shinkansen, to Kyoto. It whisked us there in just under three hours, and we had almost the whole day to view the beautiful Zen gardens and age-old temples. In one of them, a scene of *Shogun* was being filmed. Other than that it was very peaceful. We sat on a bench, a small stream running under a picturesque bridge in front of us, surrounded by trees like acers and bonsai, and many oriental flowers we had never seen before. There was the golden roof of a temple to be seen just above the treeline.

All too soon we found ourselves on a plane to Bangkok. It was a clapped-out Boeing which should have been retired many years before. It puffed and smoked its way to Bangkok. We had just a week there on the seaside. We went every year, and the gay life was easy. The first few times I was very disturbed and just not used to paying for casual sex. The money was called "a gift" by the late teen boys. This was in line with Sri Lanka, which we had visited many times before – the people were poor, and this was a kind of extra income. Refreshed by sea and sunshine, we returned to London and were greeted by rain and chilly weather.

When I was still at home, behind the Iron Curtain, I had had a pen pal from Argentina. I forgot all about him as life went on and I became too busy to get down to writing long letters ever again. His parents were Spanish and went to live in Argentina because his father had a good job offer. He and his siblings weren't even asked; they simply packed up and moved. After the father's contract ran out and he could not find another job, the packing started all over again. They moved back to Spain. My pen pal's name was Paco, a nickname for Francisco. He appeared rather saint-like, with a pleasant face like the late Seve Ballesteros.

When I settled in London, I wrote him a postcard to Buenos Aires. I did this for all my pen pals, to keep track of them should they wish to get in contact again. Someone re-addressed the card to Spain, and he wrote back from Toledo. He also was too busy to be writing long letters any more, but he told me he would be coming to England for a year or so, to live with an English family and take an advanced English course. He wanted to become a teacher, and English was essential for him to find a good job. He would live in Sevenoaks and commute five days a week to London.

After our trip round the world, Frederic went back to the mountains for the rest of the university term holidays, and I to work. Even though we were apart, we often called each other. Sometimes we had a tempestuous time and could not live together, even though we had grown into our relationship. And sometimes we could not live apart.

A few days after my arrival home, Paco rang and asked whether we could meet up some time, since he had a few weeks left before his course started. "Why not?" I am also quite eager to meet up with you," I told him, and we set a date.

When finally we met, he certainly was no disappointment – rather the opposite. Oh dear God, not again. I felt more drawn to him than I had imagined. Neither of us knew that the other was gay. He was very reluctant, even withdrawn, if our conversation came near the subject, and I played the same game. This cat-and-mouse went on for a few more meetings, until I got fed up with the situation and asked him straight out, "Are you gay?" It took him a while to gather up his wits, and he just managed a nod. I had always wished, from our first exchange of pictures, that I might be like him, and sooner or later he would have asked me the same question.

Oh yes, careful Sebastian. Are you really up to having two relationships at the same time again? I knew Frederic was seeing a student named Richard and had also had one or two other wild nights out. That went for both of us; we were burning the candle at both ends. Life seemed to be smooth and perfect.

Then suddenly the unthinkable happened. Frederic sometimes went cottaging, and he was caught by an agent provocateur and hauled in to Vine Street Police Station to sign a statement of "loitering with intent". He appeared in a few days' time at the local magistrates' court and was duly fined and humiliated.

All this happened, when we were to fly to Phuket in a few weeks' time. There was all of a sudden a downcast Frederic, and Mandryka had to help him out. There was only one thing on my mind: "Please make an appointment with your head of department and let him know what happened, in case it should ever hit the press. Much better that than being afraid, or being found out unprepared."

Again I had to ask my employer for a few days off to sort out a family affair, which was granted. Frederic and I went round and round in circles. At last he really understood. He listened to me and promised to make the appointment ASAP. Thank God, his head of department was very understanding and assured him, should he ever hear any gossip, he would be prepared to stand up for Frederic.

For the next few weeks before our departure, Frederic could not help raising the subject, since it depressed him enormously and threw a dark shadow over him. He needed help to come out of it. It was again my task to help him, and I did. Situations like this showed how sincere we were about the nature of our relationship. I knew he was a bit naughty, but one would have thought the police had other things to do than to hang around public lavatories.

This situation bonded us more deeply with each other. I did everything to help him in his hour of need. I wondered at the outset whether I should mention this at all, but dismissed the idea. Our friendship and partnership had weathered the storm; let us get on with our lives.

During this tiresome affair, I had to put Paco off and out of my mind, since he did not know I had a permanent relationship going. And who was I to judge Frederic? I also had done many things in my life, and Frederic had been my crown and anchor.

Before Frederic came back for his next term, I had to be prepared to own up to Paco that he existed and let him make the decision. Did he want to carry on or finish our relationship?

"I am too deep into our friendship," was his answer. "If you could spare one evening a week for me, I would be very happy and find an excuse for the family in Sevenoaks."

But Frederic being in London changed my feelings for Paco, and the day came when we had to say goodbye. My arms went round him for the last time, and I wiped a few tears from his face. It was not that easy to let him go. His shadow followed me. It had been a pleasure having him as a friend and lover.

Frederic and I soon got into the rhythm of our private life. The term started dismally, and it rained nearly every day. It was time for the holidays to come round and cheer us up. And yet there was a cloud on the horizon.

Our holiday destination for the last five years had been Colombo. There had been an uneasy feeling in the country ever since we first went to Sri Lanka, and slowly it started to boil over. The Tamils had been brought to Ceylon during colonial times as tea pickers, and now they demanded the right of citizenship. This was a demand the Sri Lankans did not want to grant. With the build-up of the Tamil Tigers, it looked like a civil war was not far away. If not Sri Lankan citizenship, the Tamils demanded the area around Jaffna as their separate state. That was also not an acceptable solution to the natives of Sri Lanka.

Just before we started to make plans for what we might want to see during our month there, the clashes between the Sri Lankan army and the Tamil Tigers escalated into full scale war. The advice of the Foreign Office was clear: do not travel to the country. That was our holiday destination gone.

What now? We were due to fly out on a Saturday. The warning was not given until a day before our travel. Until then, the airline with which we were going to fly to Colombo refused to give us a refund. After the official warning from the Foreign Office, they had to reimburse us. We had one day to find another destination – which we did.

On Saturday morning, Frederic and I set off to Earls Court, where young Commonwealth students on two-year visas met to pick up their mail and socialise. It was called Kangaroo Corner. It was also the home of bucket shops which sold discounted airline tickets. We made a few fruitless attempts, but finally we struck lucky with Anglo Pacific, which could offer us three seats on Garuda Airways, the Indonesian airline, to Jakarta.

"OK," said Frederic, "and what are we going to do there?"

"First we get some travel guides." was the answer. "Then we book a hotel for a few nights in Jakarta and see what we can arrange."

Unknown to us, the country had a lot of financial difficulties. On the night we travelled, it devalued the rupiah by 50 per cent. So when we arrived, everything was incredibly cheap. One guidebook referred us to a couple of agencies which were well worth checking out for additional travel within the country.

When the journey finally came to an end, we had been travelling for almost twenty-eight hours: London, Frankfurt, Abu Dhabi, Bangkok, and at last Jakarta. All we needed then was a good night's sleep. The following morning we went downtown to see if we could find an agency.

One was particularly recommended, and we made it our first port of call. The receptionist, when asked if anybody spoke English, said, "Yes. Mr. Koehler, our boss, speaks English and also fluent German. His father married an Indonesian lady."

He had spent his childhood in Germany, schooling up to O-level before the family came back to retire in Indonesia. He knew where we ought to be going and we travelled on his advice from Jakarta to Bandung, where a conference of the Non-Aligned Movement had gathered. The attendees included Indira Gandhi and Tito.

From there on we went up to the mountains to Baturaden. We were able to go with a driver and guide due to the devaluation. We continued to the Dieng Plateau, 2,000 metres above sea level.

On the way to Yogyakarta, we visited one of the oldest Buddhist shrines, the Borobudur, built before Arabian traders converted the Indonesian people to Islam. There was nobody around. We could wind our way along the Ramayana to the observation platform of the monument, which was surrounded by volcanoes, and see the mountains smouldering as if they were getting ready to have another eruption. It was a little frightening to walk on moving ground. Sub-volcanoes spat their sulphur in our faces as we walked to one of the smaller temples.

Well, Fortuna meant well by us. Yogyakarta was also a backpackers' stopover, and we enjoyed the little town built by the Dutch during the colonisation of Indonesia. From there we went on to the Brambanan, a Hindu temple, which was quite impressive, though smaller in size than its counterpart, Angkor Wat in Cambodia. We continued to Surabaya and returned by plane to Jakarta.

Mr Koehler had put a plan together for us to holiday at the seaside, in the shadows of Mount Krakatoa in the Sunda Strait, but we kept the idea for later on and went off to Sumatra, which was quite an experience. He warned us that Padang was far from developed. That went for the whole island; the coastal regions were not for foreigners since there were hardly any roads. Transport in any direction out of the town consisted of small buses, which went in one or the other direction – you just had to ask around. They left when they were full.

Apart from all kinds of livestock and the smelling salts of the ladies, there was nothing to admire. We were aiming for Bungus Beach, some ten miles out of town, but it took hours to get there and hours more on the way back to town. It was like Paradise Lost – the stretch of beach was a dream, but too difficult to get to.

Besides that, Mr Koehler had put us up in the Grand Hotel Mariana, which was all plastic and full of kitsch. The lady who owned the place was visiting her daughter in California, which accounted for the taste the hotel was furnished with. At night it got very humid. If you put the air conditioning on, it was too noisy to sleep, and if you did not, the mosquitoes and the nylon bedding got at you.

Our enthusiasm got quite a damper, and we asked to be rescued by Mr Koehler. We soon flew back and considered ourselves very lucky to escape when we did. When the plane which was to take us back to Jakarta landed, there was quite a commotion. Mrs Grand Hotel Mariana had arrived home and her entourage needed to be supervised, which she did with the greatest aplomb. Mr Koehler told us later that she had been looking forward to meeting us and had already made some plans to entertain us. Hard luck for her.

Mr Koehler put us up in Merak opposite Mount Krakatoa, as he had wanted to do originally, and we praised his foresight. We spent two weeks in a hotel on stilts. The rooms were reached over an intricate system of stairs, the logic of which still baffles me to this day. But it was cosy, and we really enjoyed ourselves. Soon it was time for our return to Jakarta, where we got ready for the long haul back home.

This interlude was particularly interesting for Frederic and me. There was a teenboys house about ten to twenty miles from town, where you could really have a good time. And since, as so often, we were the only tourists around, it meant that the place was frequented by natives as well. The talents were very pretty and very obliging. It put us in the right frame of mind and made us sorry to leave so soon.

We returned to our hotel to buy presents and have a nice lunch. Frederic's mama, of course, was travelling with us. She wanted to take her last travellers' cheques and her passport with her, which I would not have, since bike snatching was rife in all the Asian cities. And lo and behold, as we waited on the kerbside for the light to turn green, a motorbike came along and the passenger nicked Mama's handbag. We spent the last hours of the trip in a police station; it took hours filling out forms. But her passport and travellers' cheques were still in the safe. Thanks to my foresight, we were able to leave the following day

CHAPTER 14

Europe and the United Kingdom

With all the travel to faraway places, we did not forget our heritage, which after all was Eastern Europe. Vienna was foremost on our agenda. Apart from the operas, theatre, concerts, and exhibitions, it was a town where Frederic's family was at home.

It was not foreign to me either – being Hungarian born, I was as at home in Vienna as in Budapest. My maternal grandfather was stationed in Vienna for quite some time before the outbreak of the Great War. He was with the Royal Hussars and served often as guard at the Hofburg, the home of Emperor Franz Josef. He brought back my name, Sebastian, and I was always proud and thankful to him for finding such a beautiful first name for me.

After leaving the club I was recruited to run a city livery hall which I did quite successfully after a short time.

That was one of the reasons I came to England: to live in a kingdom once again. I am very fond of pomp and circumstance, and was lucky through my jobs to experience most of the British royals. That included the Queen. In one or another capacity, I was often involved in organising functions – luncheons and dinners for charities – which were supported by various members of the royal family.

I recall three particularly memorable royal events. The first one involved the Duke of Edinburgh, who was actively involved in wildlife preservation. For one of the dinners, he travelled by car to the city. He abandoned his car and arrived on foot while the members of the welcoming party were still arguing in a side room about the order of introductions.

Thank God I was at the door. I ushered the Duke into the function room on the ground floor and introduced myself. He said that he was quite relieved not to have to go through the handshaking ritual every time he went somewhere. I had my instructions, and whisky with water was waiting for him. When the Clerk of the Company and the Lord Mayor were warned, all they could do was to apologise, but he took it in good spirits. (Note that royalty had no rights in the City of London, and pro forma I had to ask the Lord Major for permission before visiting a venue.)

The first problem came to light when the guests and His Royal Highness were ushered to the first floor dining room. I was not only the steward in charge of the household but also the toastmaster. The latter should have been the job of the beadle, but I was roped in. Unfortunately our beadle had a wife with multiple sclerosis and had no one to look after her in the evenings. Professional toastmasters were shunned for charity functions, since they charged far too much for their services.

I announced that dinner was served and members of the congregation, above all His Royal Highness, should take their places. I had already been on the phone to Buckingham Palace to have the menu approved and to discover what His Royal Highness was in the habit of drinking with dinner. He sat down, and the wine butlers proceeded to serve. The Duke called me over – he wanted a bottle of light ale. That shook me into action, since beer was never served in our livery hall either before or after dinner.

I checked my watch. There was time to find the pub open round the corner. My junior butler, in full regalia, was dispatched to get a few bottles, just in case. He could not have been gone ten minutes, and came back puffing and blowing.

In the meantime, the Duke was informed by the Clerk of the Company that beer was not allowed on the premises. In defiance, the Duke had one anyway. Whew, that was a near miss!

When the Duke asked to have a look at the speech his right-hand neighbour was going to give after the dinner, he turned crimson. "Please go away and rewrite your speech," he said to the poor man. "You cannot say what you have written down." The man was a minister of the Labour Party, opposing the hunting of wild animals, which was a pet subject of his party at the time.

Well, he went away as instructed, and while the dinner was going on, he downed about half a bottle of gin with tonic. He sounded quite drunk to me when I fetched him to come upstairs. The Duke had a cursory glance at the new speech and seemed to have no objection. Dinner concluded with a toast to the Queen, and the gentlemen and ladies were given the go-ahead to smoke.

After my announcement, the speaker got up to give his speech. Unsteady on his feet, he proceeded to glide down more and more until he found himself under the table. "Quick, Steward," the Duke instructed me. "He is unwell. Say a few words and introduce me." Not that anyone at the dinner wouldn't have known who he was.

I said "I can't. I am really concerned about the speaker." I asked for a short interval while we sort out the problem.

His Royal Highness got up and said, "Since the steward refuses to introduce me, I will begin with my speech, which will be short and to the point." That was the Duke all over. Now it was on me to go crimson.

The second incident involved the Queen Mother. It was one of the few times when a royal had to use a loo. She was gone for quite a while. I spoke to the security guards, and they scuttled off to search the building. I went to talk to the chef to delay the sweet for a while. Who did I see standing in the kitchen but Queen Elizabeth, the Queen Mother, congratulating our chef on his cooking? Her lady in waiting had just popped to the loo herself and missed her royal charge on her return. In the meantime, the royal guest had found the back stairs and ended up in our kitchen. Her lady in waiting was none other than Debo, the Duchess of Devonshire, one of the famous Mitford girls.

One evening I found myself in a different hall to help out with the toastmastering. Diana, Princess of Wales, left the reception line-up standing and made a beeline for me to ask me if I had left my other job. I told her I had not. "That's very good, because I will soon have a function there again." This story circulated in all establishments like ours, and for a while the air was full of gossip and unforgiving.

Princess Diana was my favourite royal, and I was very shocked when she died while I was on holiday in Thailand.

When we got back to Heathrow, we found a country in mourning. As Tony Blair said at the time, the people's princess had died. It more or less forced the Queen to break off her holiday and come back to London. And yet the Queen's personal standard was not flying, but only the Union Jack at half-mast. For quite some time there were all sorts of rumours and speculations up and down the country. I am a great believer that there were other forces behind the fatality; she did not meet her death by accident. But for Frederic it was just an accident, and I could not mention my misgivings in his company. He was convinced it was all a figment of my imagination.

There were other occasions, I recall, when this charming lady showed how much she cared and how dear the cause of a particular charity was to her. Frederic just looked at me and shook his head. Well, he was not around in my life until I was almost 23, and there was plenty I would not tell him.

When Princess Margaret married Antony Armstrong-Jones, the Queen bestowed on them the titles of Count and Countess of Snowdon. During that time I was often in London, escort to one of the lesser royals but nevertheless part of the scene. That was quite some time after I left Finland, during the interlude I spent mainly in Freiburg. I do not remember all the details, since I blotted them out of my life when I met Frederic. Suffice it to say that I was a saleable commodity. Indeed, I was offered the job as a model for a famous fashion house during the time I worked for the club, which the club did not allow me to take on, and that was quite some time later.

All I can say is that I had the most interesting young years, and I was blessed, when that was all over, to meet someone like Frederic. I have no regrets. Life was kind to me and bestowed me with above-average looks, on which I lived for some time. It helped me to forget the years after World War II and the brutal treatment I had under my stepfather.

On one occasion, Gerald, Frederic's brother, dropped in on us on a trip from Washington to Bonn, to which he had been posted a second time. We both were very glad to see him. Frederic and I had been in conference for a while to decide on our next trip, and we needed an adjudicator. He suggested we visit the Middle East, which he knew very well, having been posted to the Lebanon, where we had visited him. I thought, "Dear God, don't let him tell us to go to Jordan." thinking back to my intense experience with the colonel which I had kept secret all these years,

Gerald actually told us to visit Syria, which he knew very well and about which he could give us a lot of advice and guidance. He was the only person I have ever known who had gone on a camping tour in the region on his own. He visited west and east Yemen on foot, and lived and slept in very friendly and hospitality-prone private houses.

When Frederic and I visited Beirut, the pot was boiling over. For two successive days, Beirut was the target of bombardment. Now and then it hit Ras Beirut and the western suburbs, where Gerald and his family lived. On the first day it happened quickly. We were in the ocean, swimming. We heard the jets roaring nearer, and then the bombs started hitting the changing cabins that were built into small caves. We were too terrified to come out of the water. That was a close shave, a bit too near for Frederic's and my liking.

When we left Beirut a couple of days later, on our way to Baalbek, I can't remember how often we were stopped by Hezbollah, factions of the Syrian military, Lebanese freedom fighters – the list was endless. On leaving West Beirut, crossing a bridge into East Beirut, Gerald commanded, "Heads down. This is the worst place in Beirut for snipers."

But driving out of Beirut was also one of the trip's highlights, with its vista of snow-capped mountains. Baalbek was the scene of a yearly festival which had been founded in 1955. It catered for almost any kind of music – soul, jazz, opera, and classical – as well as the ballet. Concerts were performed in floodlit temple ruins, the shadows of the mountains in the background.

Among the most memorable artists to perform there were Ella Fitzgerald and the Berlin Philharmonic Orchestra under the baton of

Herbert von Karajan, who both performed in the forecourt of the Jupiter temple to crowds of between 2,000 and 4,000 people. The temple site dates back nine thousand years and may originally have been dedicated to Baal, the sky god, and his consort Astarte, the first "Queen of Heaven". It was a place of pilgrimage in Phoenician times.

Leaving the town of Baalbek, we had coffee in Anja and Anjar, an Armenian settlement of displaced people who fled the holocaust of Armenia, in which an estimated one and half million Armenians died in the years between 1915 and 1923.

Gerald did not tell us when he was asked by Bonn to negotiate a UN assignment, acting for them in Bosnia. His presence and understanding of regional dialects made him an ideal candidate for the job. Later, Frederic and I thought there had been a carrot dangled in front of him to accept the post – perhaps the opportunity to become the ambassador to the United States of America. The whole family was worried about him. When he stopped over in London on his way to Bonn, we had no idea that this would be the last time we would see him.

One Saturday afternoon there was a phone call which I answered. Pam, Gerald's wife's mother, could hardly stop crying, and I could only make out that Gerald was dead. A tingling, ice-cold feeling went up and down my spine, and the feeling of an iron grip would not go away. I could hardly believe that he and his whole team crashed into a mountain in Bosnia. All perished except the crew who parachuted out as the helicopter hit. There were a lot of theories of sabotage, but no evidence that would have stood up in a court.

Before the phone call came that afternoon, Frederic and I had been down to have a bite to eat in our local pub. It was fairly quiet until a noisy and drunk crowd of Serbians invaded the pub and Frederic started to talk to them. I did not see any sense in staying on. I understood a fair bit of what was being said but did not care to get involved. So I left.

Hours passed. The phone call came. I had to go back to the pub to talk to Frederic. I got us two large brandies and asked Frederic to come with me to a quiet corner, away from the crowd, since I had to tell him something which I felt required privacy. "Oh yes," he said. "Have you come to fetch me? I know you do not like the Serbians, but we are having a lot of fun." They were talking about the past and what the future would hold for them in a country whose language they hardly spoke.

Frederic looked at me in a strange way and said, "You look upset, as if you had just seen a ghost."

"I am sorry," I said. "I have bad news for you."

"Out with it. I can hardly wait to get back to the people whose language I have not spoken in a long time."

"Frederic, there was an accident. I am afraid to tell you that Gerald is dead. Pam rang and passed the bad news on to me."

He went ashen-faced. "When and how?"

"His helicopter hit a mountain in Bosnia, and the whole delegation perished."

He started crying, and I kept up feeding him brandy until he was legless. He felt like a millstone round my neck when I pulled him out of the pub and got him home. I put him to bed just as he was, only taking off his shoes. He fell into a deep slumber. By the time I was ready to go to bed, he had not stirred or woken up. It must have been three or four o'clock in the morning when he stumbled into my room and fell flat on the floor. He tried to tell me something, but the words would not come out.

For a short time the family became close again, before going their own ways as they had always done. But the grief lingered on. It was remarkable how Gerald's wife and children coped with his death.

CHAPTER 15

The Middle East Once More
and Up to the Indian Ocean

Gerald having left us so soon in his life was a cruel twist which hit all of us. What's more, he never got a chance to tell us about Syria and the countless trips he had made there when he was stationed in Beirut. Nonetheless we were determined that we would make the trip.

Finally we got to Frederic's reading week and set off for Syria. One of our guidebooks praised the air-conditioned, luxury buses which crisscrossed the country in all directions. Damascus was the main hub. Again we stayed in one of the local hotels, quite near the mainline station, which had seen better days, judging by the fading gold decor and the blind mirrors. We must have been looking bewildered when we came down for breakfast in the morning, for a lady in a chador pointed to the dining room and left a handful of boiled sweets on our table. The service was almost non-existent, and we made do with the food presented to us.

Later on we went to reception and enquired how best we could get to the bus terminal. "Why so?" asked the receptionist.

"We would like to put a tour together to see all the sights we came to see during our time in Syria."

As it happened, the hotel had a retired member of staff with an old Mercedes who would be only too glad to show us Syria, if we could settle on a price which suited both parties. When we met, he was a pleasant

Middle Eastern gentleman, and after a fairly short consultation we agreed on a price. To toast us, he took us to two sidelined carriages of the Orient Express, which had terminated in Aleppo, in the north of the country. The carriages were now a bar, and a huge, polished dining table welcomed any reveller, foreign or otherwise, to have a drink. He also gave us detailed instructions for finding a restaurant about fifteen minutes' walk from the hotel, which he was sure we would like. We agreed to have an early start the next morning, about six o'clock, and he would show us far more than we would have been able to see with the buses.

For the rest of the day we went through the souk, which was one of the most oriental we had seen so far, and on to the Umayyad Mosque, with its priceless carpets and artefacts. Crossing the forecourt, we came across Aladdin's sarcophagus and strange exhibitions of life-sized puppets. The puppets were performing for a class of youngsters being taught by a *Sufi* – a Muslim teacher, usually a holy man or one leading the life of a monk. The puppets depicted many scenes of everyday life, like an ancient waxworks.

Our driver Adel, not only drove carefully, he also spoke quite good English. We became accustomed to having a roadside break every morning, when he would stop in front of a bakery, buy some pastries or fresh flatbread, and serve us coffee.

The first leg of our journey started off with travelling to the south to visit Bosra (Busra Al-Sham), whose Roman theatre is the best preserved and biggest in the whole of the Middle East. Due to its situation in a desert, it was buried for hundreds of years until excavation began in 1947, ending in 1970.

On the way there we stopped at a small museum which was displaying five or six complete Roman mosaic floors. There was also a mosque, Suyydiyah Zaynab, dedicated to the Prophet's daughter Zaynab. It was there that Frederic and I saw flagellants for the first time. These people had blood pouring from their bodies where they had struck themselves, chanting "Allahu Akbar". It was horrible just to watch, and we quickly made our exit. Adel assured us that flagellation was outlawed in Syria, but this mosque was frequented by Iranians, and that kind of self-punishment was still allowed in Iran.

The following day we visited Palmyra, a former Roman city with a temple over 2,000 years old. At the entrance we saw a large, stone-walled chamber with columns outside. The vast building was probably built during Solomon's time and may be the one mentioned in the Bible as part of Solomon's kingdom. It was such a pleasant day that Frederic and I lay down in the high, coarse grass. Holding hands, we looked up at the high columns and the blue sky with hardly a cloud passing by. We were happy there and shared our feelings and well-being.

Further north we came to Homs, a town with an ancient irrigation system of water wheels not altered since biblical times. The air at the restaurant terrace, where we had an early dinner, was soothing and refreshing. Adel even picked dessert for us – the grapes which were part of the latticework roofing the terrace. The following day we found ourselves opposite Krak des Chevaliers, a Crusader castle, lovingly restored, which warranted the high entrance fees. Hafez al-Assad, then the ruler of Syria, kept all ancient monuments and buildings in a pristine state. When we got nearer, the cobblestoned entry to the castle and its winding way inside seemed very present, as if a Crusader might ride up and dismount within the higher-lying courtyard. This called for another little siesta outside the castle walls, and we watched many beautiful butterflies winging past us.

Further on we went through an area with beehive houses. They were earthen built with domes made of clay and straw to keep the heat out in the long, hot summer and the cold away in winter. We were asked by the owner of one of the beehives to come in and have a cup of mint tea. The whole family assembled on the *minderluk*, staring at us. They were so remote, away from the beaten tourist track, that they rarely saw any Europeans at all.

Finally, we saw Aleppo, the largest city in Syria. It was full of beautiful Turkish houses with latticework, busy souks, and mosques. Of course it was a must to stop at Brown's Hotel, where the plumbing roared no matter which loo you used. The bar was something out of Aladdin's cave, its flocked, dark velvet curtains matching the wallpaper. There were lots of blind mirrors and shabby furniture painted gold. The most interesting item, however, was a picture on the wall – actually a bill made out to Lawrence of Arabia, which he conveniently forgot to pay, never to return.

On our way back to Damascus, we saw from the top of a hill a working caravanserai, where weary travellers could rest. The animals in front and the sleeping area behind were completely safe. This type of inn was frequented as a stop from and to the Silk Road.

I cannot understand how someone like Assad's son can be so vile and evil, misjudging his own people. They have had just about enough of him, as have many other Arab countries of their dictators that were involved in the Arab Spring.

CHAPTER 16

The Ceylon Years

Some years before we embarked on these other visits, our Ceylonese friends urged us once again not to forget Sri Lanka. And for about five years we spent our winter holidays just like our summers, at the Mount Lavinia Hotel in Colombo. This was a haven for Frederic and me. We learned, from other people and a certain gay bible, that there was quite a lot going on there.

Mount Lavinia was the former residence of the Sri Lanka's colonial British governors. It had had some modifications done and opened as a hotel. It was situated at the end of Galle Road, perched on a rock with an unlimited view of the Indian Ocean. One could watch the most spectacular sunsets. From the terrace of the swimming pool bar, the sun just dropped into the sea, and within minutes night fell into the ocean.

Some encounters just happened. We had hardly arrived before a lifeguard at the beach had a little fling with me. Frederic hadn't quite made it and was a bit sour. He made up for it in meeting a guy who knew safe houses and had a string of teen boys on hand, should you feel the urge. He was always to be found on the beach, doing brisk business. This was the first time that I paid for "a present". They well needed it, since the country had stagnated under S. Bandaranaike's brand of communism.

Our encounters on the beach or in the cheap, run-down hotels were quite interesting at first, but the second time we arrived for a holiday, I asked Frederic if we could go to the Galle Face Hotel. We could just as well watch the sunset from their terrace, and also see what was happening around the former polo green. The first thing we saw was David Bailey shooting pictures for some fashion magazine or other.

At the first sundowner on the green, there was nothing happening. The talent we saw, we were not fond of. But the third or fourth time we encountered a couple of very good-looking guys circling the green. Frederic told me, "I think we are in business. Let's pay and follow them around the green." Their names were Ruvan and Lakshan. I fancied Ruvan and Frederic Lakshan. Good that I fancied the first one and Frederic the second one. They were well spoken and came from good families. Had their parents known where they were hanging out, they would certainly have forbidden them to go out for a while.

Well, we were very lucky with our friends. First of all, they did not want any presents. Second, we were invited to their house for dinner. The respective parents had no objections; so far as they knew, we just accidentally met, and the age gap was not too great. Since Frederic's mama was still with us, she was invited as well.

Somewhere along the line the young men persuaded their parents to show us as much as they could of Sri Lanka. Later on they were going to study in Oxbridge; at present this was still a few years off. They became our permanent friends when we holidayed in Sri Lanka. All was above board, since sometimes Mama had her lady friend, the one who had given me sanctuary during our fathers' witch hunt, joining us.

Our first excursion took us to Nuwara Eliya, referred to by the natives as Nureilia. The plateau is about 1,900 metres high, and the train journey is nine to ten hours from Colombo at sea level. Ruvan and Lakshan got us six seats in the observation carriage at the end of the train. We first travelled along the coast, with green paddy fields on the opposite side, through palm groves and rubber plantations. Slowly the train started climbing towards the tea plantations. We had a good time enjoying lunch, which our friends brought with them, since they maintained that the food in the dining car would not be to our liking. The higher up the train climbed, the more beautiful the view became.

There was a light drizzle of rain, and the vegetation became quite English, with vegetables and fruit trees we knew from home. The old town and the station still lived in colonial times, very reminiscent of Scotland. When we arrived at the hotel, they were just clearing away high tea's cucumber sandwiches and scones with clotted cream.

Since we had not too much luggage, our cases were quickly unpacked. We met in the bar, where a fireplace was roaring. It was cold, and we had boarded the train at sea level, where there was a much higher temperature. We had a few arak sours before being asked to proceed to the restaurant.

Thank God we had brought jacket and tie. Time had stood still in Nureilia, and butlers with white gloves served our dinner, which happened to be roast beef and Yorkshire pudding, with a roly-poly to follow. I found the hotel quite decadent, particularly when I and the others discovered a bedpan made of brass with a wooden handle.

As the years went by, we built some very pleasant memories of the excursions we made with our friends. One in particular was a visit to Wilpattu National Park. We saw our first tusker, tiger, and cheetah. The government lodge which we hired had an open veranda with a pond nearby. During the night, we saw all the wild animals come out of the bush and have a good drink. On one occasion Ruvan and I climbed a ladder to observe from above what was going on in one of the overgrown ponds. The platform was a bit shaky, and when I saw a crocodile with an open mouth watching us, we made a fairly quick retreat.

The highlight of our excursions in Sri Lanka was the Kandy Perahara, one of the most colourful festivals in the Asian world. Normally it takes place in August. Elephants get gathered up over the whole island for the ten-day festival. First you have the whip crackers, dancers, torchbearers, and flag bearers. Then the elephants arrive, covered in silk of all colours. In the middle, the most festive one carries on his back the tooth of Buddha, which has historically been kept at the royal palaces in a temple just built for it, following the capitals which ruled the country – first in Anuradhapura, then Polonaruva, and finally in Kandy. The tooth is brought out in its casket from the Temple of the Tooth upon the tallest elephant. The spectacle goes on for hours. Everyone is gripped by the beauty of the colourful and festive procession, which has taken place since the third century BCE, we were told.

None of us knew that, when we parted from our friends after this festival, it would be the last time we saw or heard from them. The British Foreign Office advised all its citizens to leave the country, as the war between the Tamil Tigers and the Sri Lankan army had become more serious.

"What are we going to do in the future?" Frederic asked. It was always hard for him to confront a new situation. He wanted everything to stay the way he liked, and hated anything to do with change. Well, it was out of our hands. Indeed it was hard for me as well. I can never forget the Sri Lankan ladies coming out about an hour before sunset, having a stroll on the beach in their colourful sarees, moving along with the gentle breeze off the Indian Ocean.

"Why not try Bali?" I suggested.

We finally did. Garuda was still the cheapest airline, but also the slowest in getting there. It meant another two hours' flying time, changing planes, and rechecking IDs. Bali was like Paradise – hard to get there, but worth the extra hours.

We stayed in a bungalow hotel in Sanur. Frederic's Mama had her own house frog, living under the flue of the water discharge of the air-conditioning. She could open her door and step into the sea a few metres away. The distance was even shorter to the swimming pool: we were next to. We had a noisy gecko who caught flies during the night and slept during the day.

The religion of Bali was Balinese Hinduism (a religion which is recognised by Indonesia) the Indian religion, completely the opposite of Islam in the rest of the country. You could see ladies with frangipani flowers in their hair and baskets under their arms, bringing alms to the many spirit houses dotted throughout the gardens. The hibiscus there had colours one never found anywhere else.

The temple of the wind, Tanah Lot, could only be reached during low tide. Besaki, the mother of all temples, was about a thousand metres up the slope of Mount Agung. These were the most revered temples; others were much smaller and really just for the natives.

There were many dances, which were accompanied by gamelan music, one of the best known being the *kecak*. There were also quite often big funeral ceremonies with all pomp and circumstance, and many families busy with the preparation, since a single funeral and pyre was out of reach for most Balinese. The people who were to be cremated did not die all at one time; they had been temporarily buried in the interval before the ceremony. The Balinese sometimes put live chickens into their burial shrouds to make it to look as if the person were still alive.

It was a colourful procession of mixed flower floats between tow ropes attached to the dead in white body bags carriages, slowly proceeding to the funeral pyres. The Balinese really believed that death was not an end but a new beginning. Once the pyres were extinguished, the ashes were scattered in the sea. Nothing was done just for the tourists; the cremations were real.

But the beaches were just for *farangs*. Staying in one of the hotels was like being in a ghetto. The staff disappeared at the end of their duty and there was nowhere to go other than a beach bar or an open-air restaurant. The same thing happened in Penang, on its beach called Batu Feringi. The natives lived elsewhere, and the tourists were housed too far away to get into town. The only alternatives were to stay put or visit another hotel, where the situation was the same as in one's own hotel.

Frederic and I went a few times to Kuta on the other side of the island, where a lot of Aussies stayed. The surf was quite impressive, and it had lots of bars and clubs frequented by the younger crowd. In 2002, a suicide bomb went off in one of those bars, Paddy's Pub. It killed two hundred people, with the highest number, eighty-eight, being Australians.

Frederic and I had re-established an understanding yet again. We often sat on the barrier reef about five hundred metres off Samur Beach, our legs in the water, enjoying Bali's balmy wind. We were nearing twenty years plus together, and our feelings for each other were just as real and true as if we had met yesterday. He was a very special person. I do not think many people have had my luck in being with their once-in-a-lifetime love for so long, particularly in gay life. We still enjoyed horseplay and often knocked each other into the water. The days were magical and beautiful, carefree. We were looking forward to being together for another twenty years.

We also revisited Java, Yogyakarta, the Borobodur, and the Brambanan. Commercialism had touched the relics of the past, and you could not go unhindered wherever you wanted. Just like Egypt you had to park about a mile away and take a noddy train to the sight. But the magic of yesteryear hung still in the air for Frederic, his Mama, and I.

Presently, when I am writing these lines, Chopin's *Romance Larghetto* is playing in the background. We heard it so many years ago in the former Yugoslavia, and it makes me quite nostalgic. Why could time not have stood still? Why could we not go back to the beginning of our affair? In a way, for Frederic and me, time did stand still; it just became a bit more mature than it was in the beginning.

"Hush," said Frederic once, "there is still so much to look forward to. Imagine what we can do together, just you and me."

Sometimes, when he was in a jocular mood, he used to tease me, "Whomever we meet, in the end you associate a piece of music with them." One is the "Finlandia", which marks my adolescent year with Maja. Another was for our lady friend Marta in Budapest, whom I best remember with the intermezzo "Cavalleria Rusticana" by Mascagni, since this was playing on the radio when we visited her for the first time. Whereas when I think of Frederic's mama, it is with her most beloved music, the *Deutsche Messe* by Schubert. The list is endless. I am happy to have these memories, and they are still as fresh as they were many years ago. And since all my favourite music is on my iPod, it is not too difficult to revisit them.

And all this happened to a boy who was born into a farmer's family in deepest Hungary. As they say, "Maybe the first years were hard, but later on, you made as much of it as you could."

Chapter 17

Tibet

Using Pattaya in Thailand as our base, we travelled many times to other destinations. The best excursion we ever experienced was to Lhasa, Tibet. There was a company called Diethelm in Thailand with a good connection to Kuoni, the long-haul flight company. When we approached them, the price tag was a bit hard to swallow. But they gave us the opportunity to see a country which was annexed to China, but still fighting to become a free nation. The Dalai Lama is still Tibet's spiritual leader, living in exile in Dharamsala in the Indian Himalayas.

Let me briefly describe how the travel company worked. The minimum number of travellers in a group was five. Three Japanese citizens were scheduled to travel with us, but they could not make it because one of them got seriously sick. Just the two of us left Thailand on a late flight.

A go-between waited for us at Kathmandu airport. He took our passports to the resident consul of China and had them stamped and signed with the visa to fly into Lhasa. So far so good, but then the immigration officer questioned whether he ought to let us travel on. A long consultation took place, which made the other travellers in the airport nervous and ill-tempered.

In the end, we were allowed in. On the Tibetan side, we were greeted by a lady officer in a costume you would associate with an operetta: all blue, with plenty of gold buttons and epaulettes. "I see that three others got conveniently sick and cancelled. Now is this not a coincidence?" she asked. We kept quiet and put on our best smiles we could muster, till we were safely outside the terminal building.

There our guide was waiting: Tiki, who took Frederic by storm and vice versa. It was the first time I had seen Frederic like that. Now it was me who had to put up with a situation. It was quite alien to see Frederic with a lady, and it lasted till we left Tibet.

On the long drive from the airport, Tiki and Frederic talked about the Tibetan religion. Everything felt like it was happening in slow motion. The altitude made us light-headed, and there could be no outing on the day of arrival. We were urged to take some rest and drink plenty of green tea. Just the thought made me nauseated. This is one of the reasons why the Chinese will never be fully integrated into Tibet. A lot of them can't function properly in the altitude.

Beijing did not recognise any time zones in China. We often went to bed with the sun still bright, and got up in the night and waited for dusk to lift. But these were only slight irritants, since we were on holiday and it did not matter to us.

Visiting a museum of ancient medicine, which is partly still revered to this day, we met a young Chinese doctor. He had overheard us talk in English, and approached us. It turned out that he was leaving the following morning, since he could not work under these conditions. This most of all pleased Tiki, who had attended university in Beijing and come back to Tibet with a healthy loathing of anything Chinese.

Of course the Potala Palace which dominated the skyline of Lhasa which's top was reached on steep staircases with many murals of Buddha's and Bodhisasattvas which accompanied the visitor to the top floor where the Dalai Lama had his small sanctuary with a separate prayer room. The Summer Palace of Norbulingka was also a must, since this was the place where the Tibetans built a human shield six to ten deep against the Chinese army for the Dalai Lama to escape into the mountains with a two hour advantage. We also met a troupe of musicians whose instruments and songs reminded us of the troubadours of the European Middle Ages.

There also was another reason to go to Tibet. Frederic and I had read the memoirs of Heinrich Harrer, an Austrian mountaineer who lived with the Tibetans for seven years. His skill in foreign languages was very much in demand; even the Dalai Lama used him as an interpreter.

The altitude played tricks with Frederic and me. "Look Frederic, over there," I said once, pointing toward someone among a dozen visitors. "Is that by any chance Mucki?" (That was the name of his friend who gave me cover during the witch hunt by our fathers.)

We went nearer to see who she really was. She seemed to be receding. By the time we got to the point where she had been standing, she had faded away. This was in the courtyard of Sera Monastery, where the young student monks had heated debates about Buddha's teaching –quite noisy, but interesting to watch. The outer precinct was dominated by stray dogs. Tiki told us that these were the reborn students who had turned out badly in life, so their souls could not rest.

Every day we looked forward to having a couple of beers at an establishment overlooking Barkhor Square. This was quintessentially a Tibetan affair with a very colourful market. The Tibetans wore traditional dress, and everywhere were buntings and bells chiming in the evening breeze. On every corner of the square was a large incense burner, shrouding the market in a light haze. We could see the entrance of the Joghan Temple, where crowds of believers slowly crouched on their knees, asking Buddha for forgiveness of their sins. The prayer mills were very busy, falling in with the bells rattling away in the distance.

Frederic and I were sorry to leave; the week was over so quickly. We bought a small carpet at a nunnery in town, where we could see the nuns weaving on antiquated looms and smiling happily amid their toil. We also tried to talk to Tiki about sky funerals, but her only comment was, "Please do not talk about these. They are very gruesome affairs."

It was a fair morning when we left for the airport, each of us taking a bit of Tibet with us. That trip would not be rivalled in our many travels of the world. It was an unforgettable experience in many ways.

Even the journey home was hopeful. Frederic was due to receive an associate honorary membership in the Royal Academy of Music, and I was to start a new post as the steward of a worshipful livery company in the City of London. We both had something to look forward to.

Our love prospered, and happiness was never far away. We both had achieved more than we dared to hope in a foreign land.

When I began my new post, there was no infrastructure in place at the livery hall. It was up to me to build a household of permanent staff and casual labour. It was also my job to let the hall out commercially (after the clients had been vetted by the court and the master) during times when the livery company did not need the facilities. The undertaking was a huge success. I turned over more than a million pounds and made a substantial profit from the City banks, which were awash with money before the fatal Black Friday.

The senior butler was chosen. The chef had been hired from a club in the West End. It remained to choose the junior butler. The chef knew a lad, about 21 years old, in St Albans. He asked me to interview him, since he had done some waiting and was at a loss right then for suitable employment.

His name was Peter. He was one of the best-looking young men around. I said to myself, "No, Sebastian. No. You dare not start anything." But it was hard. He was tall and blond, with the face of a cherub. He would have done well as Siegfried in Wagner's opera, Germanic-looking to the core. Of course I employed him – after he also made a good impression on the clerk of the company, who had to vet all my appointments. Peter was to start in two weeks' time.

Meanwhile life was busy for me, implementing all my goals into reality. It was a hard task, but I enjoyed every minute of it. And as long as I reported daily to the clerk and did not upset any of his pet administrative staff, we all got on fine with each other. Since I was the only one with formal hotel training, contradictions were kept to an acceptable level. "Slave driver" I was called now and then, when the staff did not get away with laziness or sloppiness.

Peter was a good pupil and picked things up very quickly, whereas the senior butler – goodness knows why I employed him – was often missing for hours. He was a lazy sod and we had many run-ins, since he maintained I was working the staff too hard, including him.

The butlers' dress code was a standard morning suit or, for festive occasions, livery in sky blue with lots of brass buttons all over. Peter loved it; Barry, the head butler, hated it. For me it was a different story. I wore a morning suit first thing. Then, if the court had lunch, it was a cutaway. In the afternoons or letting out the hall (which was called lenthall), I had to wear livery, as well as for many charitable functions. In the evening it was a dinner jacket or white tie when the court had one its formal dinners with the loving cup ceremony or other important events. Getting dressed often kept me more busy than the actual work. I had a little flat at the top of the hall, where I could withdraw and go about my business of changing.

Along the corridor next to my flat were changing rooms and showers for the butlers. One evening there was a knock on my door. It was Peter, who was quite distressed, since the shower was not working and his shirt had not come back from the laundry. "Come in and use mine," I told him. "I will also see if I have a shirt for you."

I did. The arms were a bit short, but by not folding the double cuff, he got away with it. Meanwhile I continued reading a book. I was still in my dressing gown, since it was a good hour before we had to appear for final briefing in the livery hall.

Having left his clothes in my bedroom, Peter came out of the shower with just a towel wrapped round his waist. What a sight for sore eyes. He was just too perfect. I asked him to sit down in the armchair and offered him a glass of wine to steady his nerves. I am not quite sure if they were only his nerves or mine as well. I thought, "Sebastian, tell him to get dressed and go." I couldn't. I was paralysed and succumbed to his charm.

It wasn't long before he landed next to me on the sofa. We looked at each other and kissed. I sensed he had never kissed a man before. Indeed, there was a rumour among the staff that he was engaged to be married. He was quite shy and yet had made the overture. "Oh Peter," I said, "What shall I do with you? If this leaks out, you and I are done for – do you understand that?"

"Yes, sir."

"Oh, drop the 'sir'. To you tonight, I am Sebastian."

It took all my willpower to disentangle myself from him, and I went to sit opposite him. "Peter, let's sleep on it. In the next few days, if there is nothing on at the hall, we will go out to the pub and discuss our situation. But for now, get dressed. No sign of recognition must pass between us tonight."

The day came when we were due to meet. As it had been for me with Frederic the first time, my mind was in turmoil. Peter was 21 and I was in my mid-forties. I was still very good-looking, but this boy could be my son, and he was falling in love with me.

We found a secluded corner in the pub and talked and talked. "What about your fiancée?" I asked.

"Oh, that was only a story to get everybody off the scent that I was in love with you."

He played his cards well. No matter what I said, he held steadfastly to his belief that I loved him as well. He grabbed my hands and looked deep into my eyes. "Please love me a little," he urged. "I have always known I was gay, but didn't know how or where to start until you came along. I know you will not hurt me. I have tremendous respect for you and would like to get to know you better."

"Peter, this is a very tall order. I am only human. But I hope I can make it easier for you – as long as both of us behave as usual at work. There can be no slip-up."

"I promise."

So we met properly for the first time. Since I was in charge of setting the alarm at the hall, and knew the secret passage to circumvent setting it off, I could arrange matters. I told him and all the others to beat it. Then I set the alarm, having told him to ring the bell about half an hour later, when I would let him into the hall and up to my flat.

I was busy that afternoon getting a kind of picnic meal together. The drinks were no problem, since I had to teach him all I knew about wine anyway. There were always bottles opened for lenthall, and bottles opened could not be returned. If the casual cellarmen did not get the whole lot of them, I made my claim known.

Again, Peter was a good listener and learned fast, sitting opposite me and enjoying the deli food and excellent claret. By his consumption, I gathered that he wanted it very much, but was somewhat nervous about what would come after the meal.

What happened was very tender and loving, easing him into sex with another man. Of course, I did not go all the way, since I had never liked it myself. He could find out from someone else, if he wanted to, what that was like. He had to learn how to kiss and how to give a blow job, and he was a joy to look at.

I could never tell Frederic. He, as I gathered from a gossipy neighbour, often had younger men calling on him. Good for him, since I had to be semi-domiciled in the City, in particular if we had something on in the evening and I could not go home.

After Peter had overcome his initial shyness, he was the perfect lover. As it turned out, he was also the last one in my life who went much further than a one-night stand. We met about once a week, sometimes twice. Later on we often went to a show before we got home and had our fun together.

One night I got us tickets for *Equus* by Peter Shaffer, with Peter Firth as Alan. Whom should we meet at the bar during the interval but Frederic, accompanied by a well-known tenor of stage and opera. The tenor had been a pupil of Frederic's at the Academy, and they kept in touch and met from time to time.

The glossing-over on both sides was perfect. I just feared what Frederic would say when I got home in a day or so. Not a word. Again we seemed closer than ever. Who could wish for a better friend than Frederic? There was a loving feeling which casual sex with others could not obliviate.

And yet there was a shadow hanging over us. It was hard to define where it came from and what it meant. Our easy life seemed to be vanishing. We revisited all the places where we had been extremely happy, but nothing could mask the foreboding that something awesome was going to happen in our lives.

CHAPTER 18

La Ronde

Thailand had been our base from 1980. We spent every winter holiday there, and after a while every summer for about three months. From there we would visit other countries in South-East Asia.

Our usual time to visit was coming up. We often talked about the strange foreboding. Frederic and I were not able to pinpoint where it came from or why. Our partnership was perfect. Years before, we had signed the official partnership register, which allowed our last wills and testaments to bypass our families. In the event of either of us dying, the other would inherit the estate.

Our first excursion was a visit to Burma. We stayed at the Inya Lake Hotel, which stood in roughly forty acres of parkland bordering the lake. On one side was the official government villa for visitors; on the other, the home of Aung San Suu Kyi. Along this stretch of water, which was floodlit, it was strange that an American could swim from the guesthouse to Suu Kyi's compound without being seen, as one, it seems, did.

We often sat in the bar overlooking the lake and commented on the quietness of the setting. We loved Yangon, where time seemed to have stood still. The Shwedagon Pagoda could be seen from any part of the city, since no skyscrapers of any note had gone up to obscure the view. Every time we visited, we paid our respects to the djinns near the main entrance and the many temples within the Shwedagon.

This time we missed the towns of Bagan and Mandalay, since we had been there before. We could not get over the number of temples which were still used for prayers. Our guide at the time said, that the total was between 1,500 and 2,000. Mandalay was a laid-back dream, in particular the large site of pilgrimage with its uncountable number of *pali* tablets depicting Buddhist teachings. Frederic and I sat on a bench in the shade of a mulberry tree and had a captive audience of novice monks, who practised their English with us. They smiled happily when we praised their skills.

Not very far away was the Glass Palace, which was featured in a most interesting book by Amitav Ghosh, about the royal family that was taken from the palace and shunted around various places in India. When Frederic and I made an attempt to visit it a third time, we were turned down; it seemed we would have been there once too often.

Our little circle, our La Ronde, seemed to be in danger of breaking down. Even meditating in Luang Prabang could not help us anymore. There were times when we stayed in the guest quarters of the temple and spent more than a week in meditation, trying to find peace within ourselves. Frederic and I often talked about our thoughts. Sometimes the sky darkened, trying to tell us something, perhaps. We were searching for the landscapes of our souls. The town of Luang Prabang came nearest, with its dramatic backdrop of mountains and the almighty river Mekong flowing down rapidly towards Thailand and Vietnam.

It was very easy to fall in love with Luang Prabang, which is situated in north central Laos. Everybody went about their business in a quiet manner; loud voices and hooting car horns were a distinct rarity. Only the temple bells and gongs marked the monks' days, and the natives seemed to fall in with their routine. Whichever way you walked, there was a temple nearby, and the monks in their bright yellow habits could be seen everywhere. It was worth getting up early in the morning to watch the monks line up to receive alms from well-situated ladies of upper society.

Frederic and I often went to one of the open-air restaurants to have a meal and stay on with a good bottle of wine – a legacy of the French colonial administration. Sitting on the embankment of the River Mekong, we talked about us and our love. Then we made our way to the hotel, which led us through the night market that sprawls over the old city and into many of its side streets.

But the highlight was always our boat trip to the cave temple. The Mekong seemed to have sliced its way through solid rock and stones, which reached a height of thirty to fifty metres. On one of the bends, we usually stopped and had a picnic lunch and a nicely cooled glass of wine. On the way we could see the pagoda of Pussy Hill, with its golden dome flickering in the sun.

We felt at home at the Villa Santi, which had been the home of a princess. She had given up the villa and lived in a new wing of the hotel. The food in the restaurant of the old building was a blend of French and Laotian and just wonderful; they even had their own cuvée of claret. These quiet and tranquil times were very soothing. We somewhat forgot our cares and returned to Thailand relaxed and happy.

Another magnet was Vietnam. We did not like Ho Chi Minh City (Saigon) very much, but fell in love with Hanoi and Hue, Hanoi in particular, since the old city is still as it was under French colonial rule. On the periphery of the old town stands a copy of the Palais Garnier, the opera house in Paris.

We always stayed at the Hotel Metropole, which opened its doors in 1902 and belonged to two French brothers. It was a very elegant hotel with facilities to match. Down from our room was a suite where Noel Coward stayed many times. Our preferred room had a giant Jacuzzi and a monsoon shower in the bathroom. There was a Récamier or day-bed in the alcove of the bedroom which was Frederic's favourite.

During summer, the weather was very humid and almost too hot. Like clockwork, a monsoon shower would build up towards afternoon, often with lightning and thunder. On one of these occasions it was particularly noisy, and Frederic moved closer to me, holding tight. "Sebastian, the shadows are here again. Please, Sebastian, send them away. They want to tell me something, and I am so afraid."

I held him, and we both fell into a light slumber from which we arose more tired than we were before. There was only the one thing for it: now that the air had cooled down a little, we took a stroll to Hoan Kiem Lake, the turtle lake, which was surrounded by flame trees and weeping willows. In the middle was a small Chinese pagoda. Legend had it that the lake had a turtle living in it, which was said to be more than five hundred years old. Highly unlikely, said the scientists; it might be at most two hundred years old. But it does not matter, as long as the turtle protects Hanoi. It was said to bring luck to the city, and was revered by the Vietnamese.

On the last of our visits, we travelled to Halong Bay with its hundreds of limestone outcrops. We enjoyed a Chinese junk, just for the two of us. The trip was quite threatening in parts, fearsome in others, and Frederic's clouds came back. But having lunch and a few cool drinks restored our well-being.

Flying from Hanoi to Hue, the old imperial city, we used to stay at the Saigon Morin, which was of the same timeless elegance as its counterpart in Hanoi, the Mercure. We made a tour of the abodes of various emperors, their private estates and places of worship along the Perfume River. Opposite the hotel was the Forbidden City, the official home of the emperor. A lot had succumbed to the years, but there were enough restored buildings to give us an idea of what it must have been like. The entrance door had five openings. The largest one in the middle was for the emperor sitting on his elephant; the slightly lower ones on either side of it were for noblemen and their horses; and the smallest ones on the outer sides were for the common people.

Flying back from Hue to Hanoi, we celebrated Frederic's birthday in a very swish restaurant, the gourmet restaurant of the Metropole Hotel. The seafood buffet was of the highest standard. The à la carte menu was full of splendid dishes, and the wine was of French vintage, served slightly cool.

We started the evening quite happy, and Frederic enjoyed the food very much. Then there it was again, that cloud engulfing us. The apprehension deepened as the evening wore on, and I saw a few tears in Frederic's eyes. Was he really happy, or did he just act that way to please me? I will never know.

The following day we returned to Thailand. I begged him to fly home with me to see his physician. He declined and retorted, "There is nothing wrong with me, and I will not go home." No matter how hard I tried, he did not relent.

When the time came for our scheduled return flight to the UK, Frederic was getting worse by the hour. As soon as we landed, I rang his heart specialist on his private number, and we went straight to the hospital from the airport. We had known for a long while that Frederic had a faulty heart valve. His doctor had not given it too much attention, since Frederic tried to be cheerful whenever he went to see him. But now all alarm bells were ringing, and open heart surgery was scheduled for first thing the following morning. Routine surgery, we were told, and he would be out of hospital in ten days to two weeks.

Nobody can understand what we lived through in the moments after we heard the truth. The physician and the surgeon tried to calm us down, since the operation is usually successfully carried out. Frederic was put up in a hospital room and ordered to rest. A number of people came to see him: blood had to be taken, an x-ray was undertaken, and an echocardiogram as well as an MRI scan were ordered. Time was of the essence. I was deeply shocked, just as Frederic was.

Travelling home by cab, I dumped our suitcases, got things ready to take to Frederic, and had a quick shower. Then it was back to hospital. I held his hand, and he looked at me like a wounded animal. "Please, Sebastian, pray for me. I am so afraid."

Later on, after the surgeon and his anaesthetist talked to Frederic, I beseeched them to give Frederic an injection so that he would be able to sleep. My request was not rejected, and when I left Frederic, he was fast asleep.

Coming home the second time finally got at me, and I let my tears flow freely. "Sebastian," I said to myself, "you must be strong now. Frederic needs you now more than ever. You must put on a brave face."

When I got back to hospital at eight o'clock the following morning, they had already taken Frederic to the operating theatre. There was nothing to be done until he came out of intensive care. One of the nurses told me to go home and get some rest, because I looked awful after a wakeful night. She said she would ring me when I could see him.

I took her advice, but after I had had no call by two o'clock, I took off to the hospital again. After a few more hours, I was able to see him. When he heard my voice, he opened his eyes and looked at me with a shadow of a smile, happy I had come.

After a couple of days, Frederic was transferred from intensive care back to his room. I was used to organizing many things. To enable me to see him every day and still look after affairs at home, I got in touch with Leila, a Filipina, to arrange cover from noon to three o'clock every day among her friends. Even her English husband, Rodney, was roped in to read to Frederic.

To understand my relationship with the Filipinas, you must go back to the early 1970s. I was desperately short of domestic staff at the club and started importing these girls to work for me. I even went to an agency in Manila that arranged these matters and negotiated a fixed fee for every person they sent to me. I also paid their airfare, which the agencies used to inflate their profit. They made the girls pay back for two or three years till their passage was accounted for. By the time Mrs Thatcher came to power and stopped their immigration, I had processed about fifteen girls and boys. That was enough for my establishment, which went from strength to strength and allowed me to devote my time to other activities concerned in running the club.

About two years later, a girl named Leonora invited me to be best man at her wedding in Angeles on Luzon. She had been the second girl whom I had imported, and it pleased me enormously to be asked. Of course Frederic was delighted as well, and we looked our best in our *barongs*.

Many of the girls remained friends, but first among them was Leila, since I had promoted her to housekeeper before she could make arrangements to emigrate once again, this time to Canada. It was an honour when her husband-to-be invited me to the Café Royal and quasi asked me for Leila's hand, since there was no other family about.

I was their friend and yet their boss, and I believe I struck the right balance between fairness and strictness. Many years later, I was invited to a garden party at Leonora's house, where I met quite a few new employees of the club. Everybody wanted to see me since I had become a legend in my lifetime.

Most of them knew of Frederic, but whether they did or not, they never abused my trust in them. Now that I needed them, I could leave Frederic for a few hours in their care without worrying.

At first Frederic made a good recovery. I was looking forward to having him at home again, where I could look after him. But my prayers were not answered, no matter how often I went to Mass or beseeched God to help Frederic and me in our horribly lonely hours.

The surgeon warned me that Frederic's life was in danger. He had developed an infection in the operative wound and would have to have another operation. "But he had been doing so well – what happened?" I asked. The surgeon would not say. The stay in hospital had exposed Frederic to the MRSA bug, which subsequently invaded his body where he was most vulnerable.

Of course I had to give permission for a second operation, since I was his next of kin according to our civil partnership. I was more fearful than ever before. Frederic had his second operation.

Things seemed to have gone well again. I tended more to optimism than looking for more problems. My life went on the back burner; Frederic in hospital became my sole life and worry. I went to see him every day and prayed for him to get better.

He had entered hospital on 1 September, and we were near Christmas by now. The winter was forbiddingly grey and there was a lot of snow about, which often stayed for longer than a week. Frederic made his second attempt to recover. I took him in a wheelchair round the hospital and outside. He put on a bit of colour and looked not half as bad as after the first operation.

A few days before Christmas, they moved him to the heart ward. He was allowed for the first time in month to have some light food and to drink as much water as he liked. The improvement went on through Christmas. We celebrated with a mini tree and some home-baked Christmas cookies.

On Boxing Day, I had a call about one o'clock in the morning to come immediately. Frederic had taken a turn for the worse, and they feared for his life. I jumped into action. Since I could not get a minicab, I simply rang the doorbell of a neighbour where I saw some light in the house. I explained what had happened, and he drove me to the hospital.

The door of the hospital was locked at that hour, of course. What now? I gathered my wits and took the route to Accident and Emergency, where a kind nurse opened the door for me to get into the building.

I could not see Frederic; he was in the operating theatre for the third time. One of the wardens said, "Why don't you go home? I will inform the staff, and they will give you a call when he comes out." But how could I? I bedded myself down in an armchair in a small waiting room next to the theatres, and I waited.

I must have fallen asleep, as the surgeon woke me up and told me, "Frederic is fine now. Why don't you go home?"

"First I have to see him, and then I will go."

Frederic looked so pale and vulnerable, it almost broke my heart. But he lived, which was the most important thing. From then on he was shunted from room to room, with spells in intensive care.

Knowing my partner as no one else did, I knew Frederic had lost the will to live. They tried giving him alternative antibiotics, but it made only a short-lived difference.

So we went through January and the beginning of February. Then I was taken into a quiet room at the hospital, and the doctor in charge told me that the situation was hopeless. Frederic had only the remotest chance of surviving.

I could not watch his suffering any longer. I came to the decision that if Frederic's begging brown eyes looked at me, I would have mercy on him and give the doctor permission to take him off life support.

It was 12.55 p.m. on 11 February 2011 when I looked up from reading. I felt Frederic's hand squeezing mine slightly. He looked at me quizzically. A shadow travelled over his face, he closed his eyes, and was gone.

EPILOGUE

I have dedicated this book with much love to my best friend, Frederic, who was also my loving partner and comrade for forty-seven years. We lived our lives to the full, and had it not been for his mama and brother Gerald, who knows how long the relationship would have lasted. I had a loving family until they died. Posthumously I must pay them my respect and praise the trust they had in Frederic's and my loving and long-standing partnership.

After Frederic's death, I was frantic in my grief. I travelled many times to the countries of South-East Asia, looking for Frederic's soul. "Please dear God," I prayed, "let me see his face again, if only for a brief moment, because I feel his large brown eyes looking for me." I never had a meeting with him in all my dreams. I am still crying for him to this day.

A few times I had asked him, "Should you die before me, where would you like your ashes to be scattered?"

"Please let us talk about it another time," was what he always said, but this other time never came.

First I went to the cemetery in his home village in Bavaria and scattered half of his ashes on his mother's grave. The other half went to Luang Prabang, where I engaged a monk to travel on the river Mekong with me and scatter the ashes, chanting prayers.

Now after three long years or more, I am going back to Luang Prabang and down to the Mekong. I hope I will be at peace with myself, just as I was a few months ago back in Bavaria, visiting his and his mother's grave.

But my restlessness remains. In late August I will spend a week in Vienna, where I did not dare to go before. When I was there the last time with Frederic, we saw *Parsifal* at the State Opera. The tenor Christopher Ventris sang Parsifal, and the following day the critics praised his flawless pronunciation of German. He was one of the singers Frederic had coached at the Academy.

This year I will spend two weeks in October cruising the eastern Mediterranean, of which I am bit wary now. It should have been on the trail of the Ottoman Empire. In November perhaps I will spend a week in Sidi Bou Said, and Christmas and the New Year in Thailand.

I was so lucky to meet Frederic and to experience the difference he made in my life with his love, trust, and devotion.

Acknowledgment

"With great thanks to John and Abel who supported me right to the end in writing my memoir".

Lightning Source UK Ltd.
Milton Keynes UK
UKOW04f0926200315

248208UK00004B/60/P